Depression Glass

Depression Glass
A Collector's guide

Doris Yeske

77 Lower Valley Road, Atglen, PA 19310

To my husband, James, who avidly shares my addictive hobby and enjoys our retirement years in a house filled with an endless variety of colorful, sparkling Depression Glass.

Without his interest, encouragement, patience and willingness to travel miles and miles in search of this glassware this book would not be possible.

Copyright © 1997 by Doris Yeske
Library of Congress Catalog Card Number: 96-71512

Designed by "Sue"

Printed in Hong Kong
ISBN: 0-7643-0210-8

Published by Schiffer Publishing Ltd.
77 Lower Valley Road
Atglen, PA 19310
Phone: (610) 593-1777
Fax: (610) 593-2002
Please write for a free catalog.
This book may be purchased from the publisher.
Please include $2.95 for shipping.
Try your bookstore first.

We are interested in hearing from authors
with book ideas on related subjects.

The photography is by Sandy Burnstad, UNIQUE PHOTOGRAPHY, 307 North Superior Avenue, Tomah, Wisconsin 54660

CONTENTS

ACKNOWLEDGMENTS

The counsel and aid of my family members, friends and classmates have been invaluable in writing this book. A special thanks to all of them for their encouragement, enthusiasm and support. I would like to thank each one in print, but with so many I will have to settle with thanking you collectively and hope the satisfaction of knowing you had a part in this book will be sufficient.

I am indebted beyond measure to Dave Marcou, my instructor for the class on "Writing for Publication," who gave me the input I needed in writing this book. His frank and constructive criticisms along with keen insight and judgment helped to make writing an enjoyable experience.

A special thank you to Ann C. Dallmann, my typist, who spent hours typing the manuscript and did such a superb job.

I also want to thank my daughter, Karen, and son-in-law, Marc, who read the entire manuscript making valuable suggestions and contributing glassware for the pictures.

I am deeply grateful to Sandy Burnstad, my photographer, for coming into my home, spending hours in the selection and arrangement of the glassware, and photographing all of this glassware in this book. She did a fantastic job.

PREFACE

This book is for anyone who loves and collects Depression Glass, one of the most popular collectibles today. This precious glassware has collectors flocking to flea markets, garage sales, auctions, and shows in search of its brilliant pieces.

In a general and comprehensive way I have tried to provide timely information on the history and popularity of Depression Glass. I have included descriptions, sources, specific pieces in the various patterns and colors, and companies with their trademarks. I have also explored Depression Glassware's attraction for the collector and provided tips for its collection and the preservation. With the intense interest in collecting, this colored glass, which sparkled in the homes of the Depression Era in the 1920s and 30s, is sparkling anew in many of today's homes. The wealth of information in this book will prove invaluable to those who collect it. This publication is an excellent guide, offering what every Depression Glass collector should know.

It is my hope that this book will provide the spark for that individual who is thinking he or she may want to begin a Depression Glass collection. Perhaps they will buy that first piece, display it in a favorite location and begin studying additional reference books.

INTRODUCTION

Depression Glass is becoming today's number one collectible. Growing from my personal experience, this book portrays its history, descriptions, sources for the collector, specific pieces with their values, and much knowledge of this precious artifact.

This book is for the collector who is curious about this memorable glassware and the Great Depression from which it arose. You will find each chapter enjoyable, perhaps a little humorous, and informative.

Now is the right time to start searching for this sparkling glassware to add to your collection. Although certain pieces of patterns are becoming scarce, Depression Glass is still available to the collectors, often at affordable prices. We must preserve this precious glassware so that it will never be forgotten and can be admired and sought after for centuries.

This glassware can never be mistaken for any other glassware produced in American history. This book celebrates its historical significance with wonderful illustrations and detailed information about the pattern, color, manufacturer and date. It also serves the collector with helpful advice and accurate prices.

Price Guide

The prices listed here are the prices found in the antique shows, flea markets, and from the dealers in the mid-west. The prices vary greatly due to the scarcity and demand. The contacts with the various dealers have helped tremendously in determining this price guide.

REMEMBERING THE GREAT DEPRESSION

"Eat it up, wear it out, make it do, or do without!" No one raised in the late 1920s or early 1930s can forget this motto. It echoed widely throughout the land, and spoke of a desperate time for millions of people who were out of work.

This was the Great Depression which meant tough times everywhere for nearly everyone. People could be seen standing in long soup lines, a very familiar but sad sight. On the street corners people would try to sell fruits and vegetables for pennies. There was a perpetual hunt for every available bargain to make the family budget stretch.

It began with the crash of the stock market in 1929. Banks closed, farmers lost their jobs and experienced horrible conditions, factories shut down and prices dropped; everyone felt the effects of the Great Depression.

As bad as things were, they got worse with the coming of the severe drought of 1933. It hit the nation with its full impact and lasted about four years. The crops were virtually wiped out and vast regions of the country seemed to have dried up. People were overwhelmed. They had nothing and all around them everything seemed to worsen. The only thing many could do was to pack up their belongings and look for better conditions elsewhere. People traveled throughout the west and south looking for work and earning meager wages as migrant workers.

Mother nature continued to deal harsh blows: severe dust storms swept across the country; and the invasion of the locusts and grasshoppers. All hope seemed to have ended. It was an extremely devastating time for Americans.

One can only wonder what kept these people going. The motto "...to make do..." certainly did apply to the people. Their togetherness was the bond that enabled them to create, improvise, and utilize every resource to provide the basic necessities for their families. Strong love, loyalty, sharing, caring, courage, self-reliance, thriftiness, and commitment to one another helped people to survive.

In the midst of the doom and gloom people sought ways to have fun and to laugh. Anything free or inexpensive was the key to their recreation. Card games became great social events in American communities. Hours were filled playing checkers, putting puzzles together, and developing hobbies. Movies were a source of diversion and escape, while the radio provided music and drama. Following their favorite personalities took people's minds off their own suffering. Some of the radio serial dramas of the 1930s have continued as television soap operas to this day.

Remember "One Man's Family"? This was a favorite of mine and one I would rarely miss. This form of entertainment was great for the housewives doing their household chores. Remember the famous movie stars Clark Gable and Carol Lombard? What drama there was back in those days! And who can forget Shirley Temple with her dimples and curls? Today we cherish the cobalt blue pitcher with decoration containing the photographic image of that popular child actress. The music of Kate Smith will live on forever.

Dances were another form of entertainment and were held in the houses and barns. Music was provided by individuals who could play the violin or accordion. Remember the "Charleston," the wild dance craze that swept the country? All of this came out of that era and helped to lift the people's spirits. Today, we still cherish all of these memories of the families that survived through this difficult period. They will always be remembered as the hardy, thrifty pioneers.

The biggest weekly event in my small town was "dish night." After viewing a double feature at the movie house for about thirty to forty cents, a beautiful colored dish was handed to you. If you were a movie fan and could afford it, you could acquire a piece weekly. Little did anyone know that they were building a collection of what is called Depression Glass today. Each plate, saucer, sherbet dish, or platter was something to look forward to. In fact, dish nights were how my mother obtained most of the dinnerware she used daily.

Growing up in that calamitous era, my husband and I have vivid memories of the hardships endured by the people in the Depression. We were most fortunate to have loving, hard working, and devoutly religious parents whose faith held our families together. Thrift was the valuable lesson that was taught to us. We enjoyed simple and plain fun through our parent's ingenuity and creativity. Among the things my husband and I will never forget are the nostalgic ice cream parlors featuring the tall stemmed glasses for the sodas and the banana split bowls for the sundaes. How we yearn for these. There were good times among the bad.

In the midst of the austerity of this period, the colored glassware we call Depression Glass was produced. It brightened that time and ours as it has become one of the most highly regarded collectible glasswares in America, admired and sought after by many in this country.

For beginning collectors of this memorable glassware, knowing the history of the era makes the collecting more interesting and challenging.

Opposite page:
Tall stemmed glasses and banana-split bowls. These were very popular in the nostalgic ice cream parlors serving sodas and sundaes. **Back row left to right:** Tulip soda glass, $8; malt glass, $8; soda glass, $6; **Front row left to right:** banana split boats, $6 each.

Shirley Temple pitcher. Cobalt Blue. Produced by the Hazel Atlas and U.S. Glass Company from 1934-1942. A premium gift.
Cobalt blue, 4-1/2", $40.

This pitcher, along with a bowl and a mug, made up a breakfast set that was given away as a premium in cereal boxes. Shirley Temple, whose image appears on the pitcher, was born in 1928 and starred in numerous movies, She is cherished for her dimples and curls. Some collectors call this a creamer, but it is a milk pitcher.

Opposite page:
Colored bowls given away on "Dish Night" at the movie house. This was the beginning of building the set of Depression Glass.

Left-Right:
   Coronation, "Banded Rib," Saxon Hocking Glass Company, 1936-1940. Pink/berry, 8", large, $9. A plain pattern, the plates have a narrow sunburst of radial lines surrounded by larger, more widely spaced lines. The border is an inner circle of rings or ridges with a plain outer band. The production seems to have been extremely limited. The open and closed handles are fascinating in this pattern.
   "Bubble," "Bullseye," Provincial Anchor Hocking Glass Co., 1940-1965. Large berry bowl, 8-3/8", $16. For young collectors, this is an easy pattern to recognize and fun to collect. The pieces have scalloped edges, centers with a radial sunburst ending in a circle of bull's eye dots.
   Floral and Diamond Band produced by the U.S. Glass Company. Late 1920s. Large berry/ green, 8", $14. This pattern is similar to pattern glass produced earlier. Designs are sharply cut and the glass is much heavier. No cups or saucers.
   Pink Depression bowl with handles, spirals going to the right with the sunburst rays in the center similar to the pattern. Twisted Optic by the Imperial Glass Company, 1927-1930, 8-1/ 2", large, $20.

Below:
Weekly additions to glassware received from attending movies. **Back row left to right:** "Bubble" saucer, $2; "Bubble" platter, 12" oval, $18; "Diamond Quilted" plate, 8", $6. **Front row left to right:** Bubble cup, $6; "Bubble" bowl, $14; Coronation, "Banded Rib" sherbet, $5; "Floral and Diamond Band" sugar, $14; "Floral and Diamond Band" sherbet, $7.

WHAT IS DEPRESSION GLASS?

The 1920s and 1930s saw the introduction of a machine made, mass-produced colored, transparent, inexpensive glassware we call Depression Glass. It was manufactured when our country was in the midst of a severe financial depression, and the name of the period will forever be associated with this glass.

How was this glassware produced in such an array of colors and unique patterns and designs? First of all, the glass was made by a tank molding process, a newly developed method of making inexpensive glass. Soda ash, silica, sand and limestone were heated in a ceramic tank to make the glass. The liquid glass with coloring agents was then forced through pipes into an automated pressing mold. The finished glass assumed the shape of the mold taking on the decorations in relief that came from the pattern or design tooled in the mold. Variations in the glassware was produced by using different mold methods: the mold-etched, paste-mold, cut-mold, and chipped-mold. Most of the glassware received its decoration in the mold.

This was colorful glass: pink, green, red, amber, yellow, blue, white and crystal. It was produced in quantity by American glass factories and flooded the marketplace in the turbulent Depression years.

Life in the Depression can be described as drab, the grayness of hard times was drabness of people's homes. Colored glassware provided a bright spot. The myriad colors, shapes, decorations and sizes of this glassware was a small relief to the austerity of the bleak period.

During the same period there was another type of glass produced. This was a finer hand-made type with exquisite etching, better quality, intense color, and clarity. This glassware was called Depression Era and covers a larger period. For all beginning collectors it is wise to know that there was another category of glassware. However, the machine-made Depression Glass is the popular and admired collectible with its rich history.

The term, Depression Glass, did not make its debut until 1970 when it then became the collector's term. It appeared first in the Antiques Trading Publication in 1969. Some of the glassware was sold sparingly at house sales and flea markets in the 1960s and 1970s. Boxes of it could be found in attics, basements, barns and other storage areas. Some of it was laid aside or even discarded. When anyone who did this learns of its value today, much moaning and groaning can be heard. A tumbler worth ten cents in 1925 can be worth $150 today. How we collectors wish we could have snatched this up!

About the time of this rediscovery numerous books appeared on the scene, as did the collectors organizations. Depression Glass became a familiar word.

Prior to all of this interest, collectors had little information to help them in their search. Rarely was Depression Glass mentioned in newspapers or magazines, or seen at shows. These pioneer collectors went to flea markets and church rummage sales and began to collect various pieces here and there. Slowly they began to assemble sets.

The striking array of brilliant colors and uniquely styled patterns best describes Depression Glass. The shapes of the various dishes produced were adapted to the needs and eating habits of this specific era. There were round shallow bowls called nappies, smaller ones for cereal and berry servings, a bowl with handles on two sides for cream soups. Plates came with six-inch diameters for bread and butter or sherbet, a large serving plate called a cake plate, a sandwich plate, a chop plate or a salver. You might have an oblong bowl for vegetables, a divided plate called a grill plate, jugs, ball jugs or tilt jugs called pitchers, a three legged bowl for candy called a comport, and reamers for juices. The terms luncheon sets, dinner sets, and breakfast sets emphasized the size for serving the meals. The color and variety of forms in Depression Glass are what attracts collectors and makes this glassware so popular.

Depression Glass is the perfect representative of the era in which it was produced.

MOLD ETCHED METHOD. Back row left to right: Cherry blossom tray, $28; "S" Pattern "Stippled Rose Band" plate, 9-1/4", $10; Cherry blossom tray, $28. **Front row left to right:** "S" pattern "Stippled Rose Band" cup, $4; sugar, $6; creamer, $6; tumbler, 4-3/4", 10 oz., $5; cereal bowl, $5; plate, 8-1/4", $6; saucer, $2; Cherry blossom bowl, $45.

CUT-MOLDED METHOD. Left to right: Diamond Quilted pink saucer, $3; bowl, $8; Luncheon plates, 8", $6; Anniversary candy jar and cover, $22; Diamond Quilted cup, $10; cake plate, 12-1/2", $7; Anniversary tid-bit berry and fruit bowls with metal handle, $13.

PASTE MOLD METHOD. Front left to right: Heritage berry bowl, 8-1/2", $36; Heritage cup and saucer, $14; Heritage berry bowl, 5", $10; Heritage fruit bowl, 10-1/2", $15; Columbia butter dish, $20; Columbia ruffled bowl, 10-1/2", $16. **Back left to right:** Heritage plates: dinner, 9-1/4", $12; sandwich, 12", $14; luncheon, 8", $9.

CHIPPED MOLD METHOD. Left: Sharon, "Cabbage Rose" fruit bowl, 10-1/2", $39.
Right: Rosemary, "Dutch Rose" amber plate, 6-3/4", $5.

The array of colors. **Back row left to right:** goblet, "Mayfair," pink, $58; pitcher, "Royal Ruby," $30; bowl, "Waterford Waffle" crystal, $12; bowl, "Bubble," iridescent, $12; pitcher, cobalt blue, $35; tumbler, green "Rose Cameo," $22. **Front row left to right:** relish dish, "Mayfair" pink, $30; sugar, Cameo "Ballerina" Dancing Girl, yellow, $18; Indiana Custard creamer, $7, sugar, $5; grill plate, Princess, $14.

The variety of shapes. **Back row left to right:** sherbet, "Spiral," $5; sherbet, "Moderntone," $14; plate, "Waterford Waffle," $11; plate, Royal Ruby, $12; plate, "Bubble," $8; plate, "Bubble," $3. **Middle row left to right:** bowl, Pretzel, $10; candy dish, 3-footed, $10; bowl, "Bubble," 5-1/4", $13; bowl, "Bubble," 4", $4; Sherbet, "Circle," $5. **Front row left to right:** bowl, Waterford Waffle, 5-1/2", $18; cream soup bowl, Moderntone, 4-3/4", $17; cream soup bowl, "Moderntone," fired on pink, 4-3/4", $5; butter dishes, "Waterford Waffle," $25, "Columbia," $20; cup and saucer, "Diamond Quilted," $13.

Chop plates. **Left:** "Floragold Louisa," 13-1/2", $23. **Right:** Windsor, "Windsor Diamond," 13-5/8", $46.

Various shapes. **Back row left to right:** comport, 5", "Miss America," $15; platter, 12-1/2", "Miss America," $15; comport, 5-3/4", "Manhattan," $33; platter, 11-1/4", "Floragold Louisa," $23; comport, 6", Cape Cod, $20. **Front row left to right:** reamers, $4-5; boat-shaped bowl, 7"x 11-3/4", Windsor, "Windsor Diamond," $34; butter dish, Depression, $20; square butter dish, crisscross, $18; reamer, $5.

Tilt pitchers. **Left to right:** "Waterford Waffle," 42 oz., $25; "Waterford Waffle," 80 oz., $34; "Manhattan," 80 oz., $45; "Manhattan," 24 oz., $33.

Types of plates. **Back row left to right:** "Princess" grill plate, 10", $14; cake plate, "Sharon Cabbage Rose," $42; sandwich plate, 12", "Queen Mary," $10. **Front row left to right:** grill plate, 10-1/2", Princess, $14; sandwich tray, 10-1/2", Cherry Blossom, $28.

Luncheon set, "Moonstone." **Left to right:** goblet, 10 oz., $19; bowl (front), 5-1/2", crimped, $9; bowl (back), 9-1/2", crimped, $20; sherbet, $7; luncheon plate, 8-3/8", $15; sugar, $9; saucer, $6; cup, $8; creamer, $8.

Dinner set, "Waterford Waffle." **Back row left to right:** sherbet, $4; plate, 7-1/8", $7; plate, 9-5/8", $11; saucer, $3. **Front row:** cereal bowl, 5-1/2", $18; salt and pepper shakers, $9; cup and saucer, $10; sugar with lid, $10; creamer, $4.

Breakfast set,"Cremex." **Left to right:** creamer, $5; saucer, $3, plate, 9-3/4", $9; plate, 6-1/4", $3; sugar, $5; cup, $6; bowl, $4.

Reamers, soda fountain glasses, and banana split boat. **Back row left to right:** soda fountain glass (malt), $8; reamer, $4; banana split boat, $6. **Front row left to right:** reamer, $5; reamer, $6.

THE POPULARITY
OF DEPRESSION GLASS

Never before has a glassware become such a great collectible. Elevated to the top of today's collecting field, the interest in this colorful, inexpensive, machine pressed glassware is picking up momentum everywhere. Why is it so popular?

Perhaps nostalgia for the days when it was first produced has helped to make Depression Glass as popular today as it was fifty years ago. This glass commemorates a link with the past. We Americans are grass-root historians and love to collect these pieces that interest us and connect us to our roots.

The interest in this glassware often stems from a piece that was inherited from grandmother or another relative. Eager to know more about this piece the quest for knowledge and search begins. The acquisition of this one item starts the collector on the search for more glassware of the same type and vintage. These treasured items that we inherit have great sentimental value.

The challenge in collecting Depression Glass is another factor in the increasing popularity. Few complete sets survived due to the ravages of daily use. Finding the missing pieces is a real challenge. Searching for the lids of butter dishes, sugar bowls, teapots, candy dishes and other items can be very difficult as most of the lids are not in "mint" condition, meaning perfect or undamaged with no scratches. Today, a sugar bowl lid can cost $1000 or more if you find it intact.

Most collectors buy Depression Glass because of a genuine love for it. The machine made mold lines, dents, ripples and other imperfections, give this glassware its special charm. The intriguing patterns with romantic names, like Starlight, Moonstone, and American Sweetheart, fascinate collectors. There are also biblical names, like Adam, historical names, like Queen Mary, names from nature, like Georgian "Love Birds," geographical names, like Madrid, and patriotic names like Miss America...enough to pique any interest or taste.

The fact that Depression Glass was given away as premiums is of interest to most collectors today. Imagine the excitement of opening a cereal box and finding cobalt blue cereal bowls, decorated with the photographic image of Shirley Temple, pulling a cake plate from a bag of flour, pouring a tumbler from a box of soap flakes. Seed companies gave glassware away when selling their brands of seed. Furniture stores would give a free set of dishes or a set of glasses with the purchase of a bedroom suite. Banks, movie theaters, and other businesses gave glassware for gifts. The premium gift was a strong incentive to buy a product.

While most collectors buy Depression Glass to fill in an old set, to create a new set, to use daily, or to display for the decorative effect, buying Depression

Glass for gifts is very much in vogue now. The gift with a history has more value, and it holds it value when you walk out of the store. Each member of my family cherishes every piece of Depression Glass given for birthdays, anniversaries, weddings, and other special holidays.

For some collectors, buying this glassware is a splendid investment. Those collectors who bought it in earlier years paid pennies for the pieces. Many would watch the market to see which patterns increased in price and popularity. They bought the patterns which demonstrated the most appeal, and sold them at a great profit at a later date. Many had their children's education in mind and began to do this in the 1980s. Their investments have paid off. Today collectors are still doing this, with some making a comfortable living by buying and selling it.

Even when the glassware was not free, it was inexpensive. Imagine buying a beautiful dish for three to four cents. Sears and Roebuck offered its customers a luncheon set for $1.99. Today we often pay as much for one plate as the original price for one set. Perhaps the original inexpensive nature of this beautiful glassware is part of its charm for collectors today.

As we become more and more familiar with this uniquely styled and versatile glassware the fascination and searching grows and grows, becoming an addiction. Eager to preserve these cherished pieces and to know more about this glassware, the driving need to find and buy Depression Glass intensifies.

As Depression Glass has achieved high collectible status among glass collectors, it is clear that there is nothing depressing about it. It sparkles anew with increasing popularity.

Inherited pieces. **Left:** "Princess," 9-1/2", hat-shaped bowl, $43. Many of pieces from this pattern were inherited from grandmother. This finely etched glassware is a beauty garnered by many collectors. **Back center:** "Cherry Blossom" tray, 10-1/2", $28. This is another popular piece with the attractive all-over floral design in the mold etched pattern. **Back right:** "Princess," 9-1/2", grill plate, $14; **Front left:** Lace Edge, "Open Lace" plate, 8-1/4", $22. **Front right:** Lace Edge, "Open Lace" bowl, 9-1/2", $26. This is the only pressed pattern of this type with a pierced or open border design. A well-known pattern among veteran depression glass collectors, with the radial-lined sunbursts, and scalloped edge. Made primarily in pink.

Back row left to right: "Moonstone" candle holder, $8; "Daisy" sugar, $3; crisscross refrigerator dish without cover, $15; candy dish and cover (cover found), $25; Florentine, No. 2, "Poppy 2" sugar, $10; Waterford, "Waffle" salt shaker, $5. **Front row:** Iris, "Iris and Herringbone" butter dish bottom, $13; Sharon "Cabbage Rose" sugar, $16; Depression creamer, $5; "Fire King," bowl without the cover, $3; Windsor, "Windsor Diamond" tumbler, $9; Patrician "Spoke" bottom butter dish, $55; "Manhattan" salt shaker, $7.

Romantic Name: "Starlight," Hazel Atlas Co., 1938-1940. The design is very unusual in this pattern with the waffle design in the center creating a striking plaid effect. The borders have cross-over stippled lines. Some pieces are becoming very scarce like the sherbets, but collecting this set is a delight. **Back row left to right:** bread and butter plate, 6", $4; sandwich plate, 13", $15; luncheon plate, 8-1/2", $6. **Middle row left to right:** sherbet, $14; cup, $5; bowl, 11-1/2", $22; bowl, 8-1/2", $11. **Front row left to right:** bowl, 5-1/2", $8. sugar, $6. creamer, $6. relish, $15.

Romantic Name: "Moonstone," Hocking Glass Co., 1941-1946. A very attractive pattern in crystal with the opalescent hobnails and rims which gives a bluish effect. **Back row left to right:** saucer, $6; sandwich plate, 10-3/4", $26; luncheon plate, 8-3/8", $15. **Middle row left to right:** sherbet, $7; cup, $8; goblet, $19. bowl, 7-3/4", $12. **Front row:** bowl, 5-1/2", straight rim, $16; bowl, 5-1/2", crimped, $9.

Biblical Name: "Adam," Jeannette Co. 1932-1934. This mold-etched pattern is one of the most complete lines of tableware made. The center has a group of alternating feathers and plumes, with wide radial ridges and rims. This feathery design made in pink and green is high quality glassware and very popular with collectors. **On edge, left to right:** sherbet plate, 6", $6; saucer, 6", $6. **On table, left to right:** butter dish bottom, $25; berry or dessert bowl, 4-3/4", $14; bowl, 9", $25; berry or dessert bowl, 4-3/4", $14; candy dish and cover, $85.

Patriotic Name: "Miss America, Hocking Glass 1933-1937. This pattern enjoys great popularity with its distinctive, easy-to-recognize sunburst of radial lines, hobnail and points. Very attractive in the original pink, a strong color. **Back row left to right:** sugar, $9; grill plate, 10-1/4", $10; comport, 5", $15; footed cake plate, 12", $26; creamer, $9; plate, 8-1/2", $7. **Front row left to right:** plate, 5-3/4", $5; four-part relish plate, 8-3/4", pink, $25; platter, 12-1/4", oval, $13.

Historical Name: "Queen Mary," Hocking Glass 1936-1940. This is a full table set with many additional pieces in a vertical ribbed design. This is an attractive set and a challenge to collect in pink. **On edge left to right:** sandwich plate, 12", $10; salad plate, 8-3/4", crystal, $5. **On table, left to right:** small pink cup, $11; creamer, pink, $7; one-handled bowl, 4", pink, $6; sugar, pink, $8; celery dish, 5"x 10", crystal, $10; sugar, crystal, $5; sherbet, crystal, $5; creamer, crystal, $5.

Geographical Name - Nature - Romantic: "Madrid," Federal Glass Co. 1932-1939. This set had a wide variety of dishes. Very few know that the Madrid molds were made from the "Parrot" pattern molds which had not been too successful. The original amber color called "Golden Glow" is very popular. This pattern is heavily reproduced today. This is an attractive mold-etched pattern in a wide variety of dishes. The sherbets are in the color of amber. Collecting this glassware is a problem since the Federal Glass Company reissued this pattern in 1976 for the U.S. Bicentennial. The new glass was called "Recollection." The glass had sharper patterns and the shades were somewhat darker. Federal Glass Co. went out of business and the Indiana Glass Co. bought the molds. They added new colors which are different from the old and the designs are different. In collecting this glassware it would be wise to know the history of this pattern. **Left:** "Georgian Love Birds," creamer, $14; sugar, $15. **Center:** "American Sweetheart" plate or salver, $25. **Right:** Madrid sherbets, $8 each.

Nature Related Name - Romantic: Left: Georgian "Love Birds," Federal Glass Co. 1931-1936. This is mold etched with a subdued classical appearance. This creamer and sugar pattern is called Georgian "Love Birds" because there are motifs of pairs of birds, with baskets in the border of the plates. This is a striking pattern. Creamer, 3", footed, $14. Sugar, 3", footed, $15. **Right:** "American Sweetheart," MacBeth-Evans Glass Co. 1930-1936. This is one of the most popular of the MacBeth Evans patterns. It is mold-etched and made in a greater variety of colors than most depression patterns. This is delicate with a neat arrangement of a center motif of festoons, ribbons, and scroll designs with smaller ones surrounding the scalloped rim. It has short radial lines to the border. The salver plate (center), 12", $25, in pink is a favorite of mine with the dainty, lacy thin glass. The 8" salad plate (at right), $9, is shown in Monax.

Give Away Premiums

"Sunflower," Jeannette Glass Co., 1920s. This is a three-footed cake plate with a stylized sunflower in the center, surrounded on the border with large flowers and foliage. This item was one of the premium gifts with the purchase of a twenty-five pound bag of flour. Also found in pink. $15 each.

"Sunflower" cake plates with matching creamers and sugars. 10" cake plates, $15 each. Creamers, $19 each. Sugars, $19 each.

Coronation, "Banded Rib," "Saxon," Hocking Glass Co. 1936-1940. This pattern is famous for its berry set that was manufactured for a "special sales" promotion. The open handles make this set very attractive. 8" large berry, $16. 4-1/2" berry, $6.

Sandwich, Indiana Glass Co., 1920s-1980s; Anchor Hocking Glass Co. 1939-1964, 1977. Some items such as the cereal bowls in crystal, green glasses, plus other pieces, were found in oatmeal boxes. The name, "oatmeal glass" was popular with this promotional pattern.
Left to right: tray, $3; sugar, diamond shape, $8; creamer, diamond shape, $8; sugar, round, $9; creamer, round, $10; bowl, 6-3/4", hexagonal, $7; bowl, 4-7/8", green, $4; bowl, 4-1/2", $4; sherbet, $9; vase, $18; tumbler, 3-9/16", 5 oz. juice, $5; bowl, 8-1/4", scalloped, $9; ash trays, club-heart, $3 each.

"Fortune," Hocking Glass Co. 1937-1938. This pattern was a promotional line with the bowls packed in cereal boxes. A very plain pattern with widely spaced radial ridges emanating from the center. **Back left and right:** handled bowls, 4-1/2", handled, $5. **Center:** dessert bowl, 4-1/2", $5. **Front left and right:** berry bowls, 4", $4.

"Old Cafe," Hocking Glass Co. 1936-1940. This is a very attractive pattern with a center sunburst surrounded by a circle of radiating lines. Made especially for premiums. **On edge, left to right:** candy dish, 8", $12+; dinner plate, 10", $35; candy dish, 8", $12+. **Front, left to right:** bowl, $7; sherbet, $7; cup, $6; candy dish in Royal Ruby, $15; berry bowl, $4; bowl, $7; cup, $6.

"Oyster and Pearl," Hocking Glass Co. 1938-1940. Very appealing in its design. the rim has double ribs with pearls in between and a scalloped edge. The bottom has the ribs with pearls in the center. This pattern has few pieces, but they are great as accessories. Smaller pieces like the 6-1/2" bon-bon and the heart-shaped jelly dishes were special premiums for the boxes of oatmeal. **Left:** bowl, 6-1/2", deep handled, $12. **Back center:** relish dish, 11-1/2", oblong divided, $11. **Right:** bowl, 5-1/4", heart-shaped, one-handled, $9. **Center:** bowls, 5-1/4", heart-shaped crystal, one-handled, $8. **Front center:** "Old Cafe," olive dish, 6", $6.

Ouide, Hazel Atlas, 1930-1935. This pattern has many different colors and designs. My father received a set in the yellow and black trim with the purchase of gasoline at the station in our small town. **Back row left to right:** cup and saucer (red), $6; sugar and creamer ("Forget-Me-Not"), decorated, $8; plate, 9", $9; creamer and sugar yellow with black, $8; creamer and sugar yellow with green, $8; cup and saucer (green), $6. **Front row left to right:** cup and saucer, $6; cereal bowl, $10; cup and saucer, yellow, black, $7.

Mayfair "Open Rose," Hocking Glass Co. 1931-1937. This pattern had more than fifty items in its set. With the purchase of cookies at the store, a cookie jar was given away. **Left to right:** deep fruit bowl, 12", scalloped, $56; goblets, $58; cake plate, 12", with open handles, $33; bowl, 11-3/4", $58; cookie jar with cover, $50.

Other Promotional Patterns. **Back row left to right:** Normandie, "Bouquet and Lattice," Federal Glass Co. 1933-1940. This is a beautifully-wrought, mold etched floral all over design. The 7-1/2" plate in amber, $8, was a premium gift by the Great Northern Products Company. The large dinner plate, 10-1/2" in Patrician, "Spoke" by Federal Glass Co. 1933-1937, $7, was made especially for a large company to use as a promotional item, possibly for a well-known flour. The Patrician butter dish, bottom only, was produced at this time in "Golden Glow," $55. **Front row:** Newport, "Hairpin" by Hazel Atlas Co. 1936-1940. Creamers and sugars, in fired-on colors yellow, white, amethyst and some pink, were given away for buying seeds from a catalog. Yellow pair **(left)**, $14; white pair **(right)**, $14; amethyst creamer **(right center)**, $12. "Aurora," Hazel Atlas Co., late 1930s creamer **(left center)**, 4-1/2", cobalt blue, $22. This item given away for a dairy mix. Mt. Pleasant, "Double Shield" L.E. Smith Glass Co. 1920s-1934, produced promotional items that were given away in various hardware stores. Sugar **(left front)**, $15.

HOW DOES ONE BECOME
A DEPRESSION GLASS COLLECTOR?

Most people like the way this glassware looks. After spotting some piece in a thrift store or receiving a piece handed down from grandmas' cupboard they are eager to know more about it and to learn what other pieces there might be. The desire to collect becomes stronger and stronger and one soon becomes totally obsessed with this glassware. The search begins.

Wherever it appears, Depression Glass is a beautiful "eye catcher." Color seems to be the one single factor that attracts the collector. Pink still reigns supreme in many of the patterns with green following closely. The array of all the vibrant colors impresses the collector and sparks the interest in searching to amass a set of this beautiful Depression Glass.

The endless patterns also play a big role in the appeal and quest for this glassware. Each newly discovered pattern appears to be more attractive than the last. With each piece you collect you become more curious about it, and the desire to find more and more is the goal. One piece simply does not satisfy the collector. The joy of ownership becomes the ultimate goal.

The passion for this colored glassware comes from its nostalgic interest, the thrill of finding the elusive piece, the pleasure in displaying the items, the joy of sharing, and the challenging pursuit. It doesn't take long for collectors to realize that this colored glassware harmonizes with even the ultra modern and can be at home in almost any setting.

As the collector becomes more and more familiar with and knowledgeable about Depression Glass, they grow to appreciate its rich, memorable history. In its illustrious beauty, the glass becomes a treasured heirloom, and the collecting of it begins to serve the greater purpose of preservation. The sets are now being passed from generation to generation as treasured possessions preserving its history and the everlasting beauty for enjoyment.

The array of pink pieces. **Back row left to right:** goblet, $9; tray, "Cherry Blossom," $28; cake plate, 12", with handles, Mayfair, $33; three-part relish plate, 10-1/2", Lace Edge, "Open Lace," $26; goblet, $9. **Middle row left to right:** bowl with spirals, $20; bowl, "Cherry Blossom," $45; bowl with cover, "Poinsettia," $35; bowl, Waterford "Waffle," $12. **Front row left to right:** sugar with cover, "Doric," $14; creamer, "Doric," $10; cupped fruit bowl with handle, $35; bowl, "Petalware," $11. creamer, "Sunflower," $19; sugar, "Sunflower," $19.

The array of green pieces. **Back row left to right:** tumblers, $10 each; cake plate stand, Princess, $20; grill plate, Princess, $14; tray, Cherry Blossom, $28; tumblers, $10 each. **Middle row left to right:** tumblers, Hex Optic, $4 each; green bowl with cover, $12; flower bowl, $20; tumbler, Bow Knot, $12; tumbler, Rose Cameo, $22; preserve dish with slotted lid, Twisted Optic, $30; sugar and creamer, Depression, $15. **Front row left to right:** sherbet, Circle, $5; Sunflower sugar, $19, creamer, $19; saucer, $2; Georgian "Love Birds" sugar, $15, creamer, $14; sherbet, Spiral, $5; saucer, Spiral, $3; Sharon "Cabbage Rose" sugar, $16.

A variety of tall stemmed goblets. The green goblets were produced by Bartlett-Collins in 1927-1930s. These were very popular for the sets of dishes. $10 each. The pink goblets are very elegant with the vertical lines and etched design. $12 each. The crystal goblet is "Ring" "Banded Ring," Hocking Glass Co. 1927-1932. $7.

HOW I BECAME A
DEPRESSION GLASS ADDICT

The collecting instinct has always been in me, and grew stronger and stronger as my family left the nest. Even before I collected it, I admired beautiful glassware, especially table settings and displays in the store. The brightness of the colors and the unique shapes of the colored glassware intrigued me from my first glance. I became totally fascinated with anything that resembled Depression Glass. With its strong appeal, I would always think how nice it would be to have this piece or that.

A uniquely patterned pink bowl on top of my mother's sewing machine was what started me on the journey of collecting Depression Glass. For a long time I had admired this bowl for its color and the unusual pattern. As I inquired about it, my father informed me it had been my grandmother's and, if I liked it, to take it home with me. He also explained that the bowl was part of a whole set and the various pieces were shared within the family.

Cherishing this bowl I had to know all about it and in the process of finding out, I got "bit" by the Depression Glass bug. This piece turned out to be the 8" curved in top bowl in the "Miss America" hobnail design with the sunburst center, produced by the Hocking Glass Company in 1935-1938. "Miss America" is one of the top patterns, or a "star" in Depression Glass. This bowl is my pride and joy for display purposes only and has a pretty rose pink color. Pink, being my favorite color, I started to search for anything pink. This became more and more fascinating and now I am a collector of all Depression Glass and love it all.

While browsing through a small mall a few months later, my daughter and I spied a pink center handled dish in the window at a thrift store. Looking at it, the color and shape impressed me and so I went in and purchased it. Later, I discovered it was a bon-bon, a small uncovered candy dish very popular in the Depression Era and very popular with me today.

A short time later, I inherited from my neighbor lady another pink piece, an elegantly designed, footed boat-shaped bowl with turned-up sides. This unusual style overwhelmed me and I became more and more fascinated with the colors and shapes of this glassware. Later, I found out that this unique bowl was called a twelve-inch muffin dish. I would never use it for that purpose but it is ideal for fruit. This, too, is on display.

Later on I was again fortunate to inherit an exquisitely designed luncheon set in a soft yellow, topaz color, from my neighbors, an older couple whom I had cared for. This set was something to admire, a real beauty known as "Jubilee" in the elegant glassware produced by the Lancaster Glass Company in the early 1930s. Searching for the additional pieces in this pattern has been a challenge but I have been lucky to find rare pieces like the candlesticks, the two-handled cake plate, and the sandwich plate.

Collecting this glassware became more and more exciting and the search expanded to include all of this beautiful, colored glassware. My intense love and extreme interest in this glassware became an addiction.

While searching, I started researching. Learning about this precious glassware is the big challenge. It is almost as much fun as finding the one specific piece which I call the "big find." Reading extensively on this subject is very rewarding to me. This yearning for more and more knowledge about Depression Glass became more and more addictive.

The display of this sparking glassware throughout the house reveals my profound love for all Depression Glass. The numerous shelves, hutches, and curios have become something of a museum. All of this glassware gives our home a personality reminiscent of the typical Depression Era look. I collect it for its aesthetic appeal and the historical significance, having grown up with it in the late 1920s, 1930s and 1940s. My favorite glass is that of the 1920s and 1930s vintage. However, I am attracted to the 1940s, 1950s and 1960s glass, which is becoming extremely popular.

I use much of my glassware. It is great for special dinners, luncheons, and especially the holidays. Around December 1st, Royal Ruby and Forest Green make their annual appearance in our home. Red and green vases adorn the window sills and fireplace, and the table displayed with the red and green dishes create a very festive scene.

As my friends and family members view and browse through the rooms of our house they become truly fascinated with it and before long they become hooked, too.

"Miss America". The 8" curved in top bowl with the hobnail design and with the sunburst center. This bowl is still my favorite in the strong pink color. Very attractive to display. $72.

"Bon-bons". These were very popular in the Depression era and are popular with me today. These small uncovered candy dishes are quite versatile for serving snacks, and particularly attractive with the center handle. **Left to right:** center handled, $12; two-handled, $15; center-handled, $20.

"Jubilee" luncheon set, Lancaster, early 1930s. This is an elegant and very delicately designed glassware in a soft yellow, topaz color that has become a collector's dream. This set has an elegant flower and leaf design containing 12 petals with open center. Cups, $16 each. Saucers, $7 each. Creamer, $23. Sugar, $23. Plates, 8-3/4", $16 each. Tumblers, 6", 10 oz., $43 each.

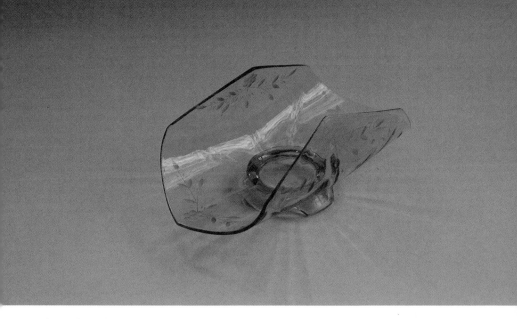

Fruit Bowl. A pink, elegantly designed footed boat-shaped bowl with turned-up sides. This unique bowl was called a twelve-inch muffin tin. This is my favorite fruit bowl. $35.

"Jubilee" candle sticks, two-handled cake plate, and the rare pink sandwich plate with the pink sugar and creamer. These pieces I acquired through a long, thorough search of antique stores, shows and flea markets. It is a real challenge to find the additional pieces. Candlesticks, $160-175. Two-handled cake plate, $47. Sandwich plate, 13-1/2", $75-85. Creamer, $30-40. Sugar, $30-40.

"Silver Crest," Fenton. These two tid-bits, two-tiered ruffled plates, were my "finds" at a Good Will store and a small antique shop. **Left:** tid-bit, two-tier luncheon/dessert, $46. **Right:** tid-bit, two-tier luncheon/dinner, $47.

"Silver Crest," Fenton Co. 1943 to present. This is a pattern of the 1940s, 1950s, and 1960s which is extremely popular and came in a great variety of shapes. The demand for this glassware is tremendous and still being produced. **Back row left to right:** vase, $12; comport, $18-20; bowl, $15-20; comport, $25-30; comport, $10-15; bowl (on edge), $30; sherbet, $11. **Front row left to right:** bowl, $18-20; banana boat, $50-60; comport, $18-20. Prices vary.

"Silver Crest," Fenton Art Glass, 1943-Present. Very popular at the present time for its crimped and ruffled edging. This cake plate was my "steal" at a garage sale. $39.

Array of Forest Green and Royal Ruby vases. The assortment of these vases in Forest Green and Royal Ruby were produced by the Anchor Hocking Glass Company in various sizes and styles. The 4" ivy ball vase called "Wilson" pictured in the middle of the front row contained a citronella candle lit to scare away mosquitos on patios or porches. These were used primarily in the southern states. This explains why they are quite available. The other small vases have a beaded or flared top. Vase, $4. The 6-3/8" bulbous vases with the rings around the center called "Harding" are very attractive for display on window sills. The 6-1/2" full vases with the plain narrow tops are also nice to display. These are called "Coolidge." These vases make their annual appearance in December, proudly displayed on window sills, fireplace and tables. Prices vary from $4-15. Vase, 6-3/8", $6. Vase, 6-1/2", $6. The narrower vases with the uniquely flared tops are neatly shaped and easy to display. The 9" vase, called "Hoover," is the ideal flower vase. These are so festive looking with white flowers. Narrow vase, 6", $6; 9", $10-15.

Opposite page:

This is the table setting of Forest green manufactured by the Anchor Hocking Glass Co. 1950-1957. What is so interesting and baffling about this pattern is that, even though it was being made later, some of the pieces are difficult to find. The rectangular platter and the square dinner plates have become the elusive pieces. The color appeals to the younger collectors. My family loves this glassware for Christmas. This set too, is very festive. Dinner plates, 9-1/4", square, $28 each. Cups, $6 each. Saucer, $2 each. Tumblers, $6 each. Sherbets, $7 each. Dessert bowls, 4-3/4", $5 each. Bowl, 7-3/8", $13. Bowl, 6", $15. Bowl, 5-1/4", $28. Cherokee Rose candlestick with green candles, (center), $35.

This is the table setting of Royal Ruby manufactured by the Anchor Hocking Glass Co. in 1938-1960s. In 1938, Royal Ruby started its big promotion with tea bags packaged inside of a tumbler. From then on this glassware became very popular. Round dinnerware pieces are from the early production. Many accessory pieces were made like ash trays, bon-bons, punch bowl and cups, vases and relish dishes. There are three items that are very hard to find, the oval vegetable bowl, the 11-1/2" salad bowl and the 13-3/4" salad plate. Not all glass in the red is Royal Ruby. Only the glass produced by Anchor Hocking can be called Royal Ruby. The Royal Ruby table setting is lovely for Christmas festivities. Admired by family and guests. Plates, 9-1/8" round, $12 each. Cups, $7 each. Saucers, $3. Bowls, 4-1/2", $6 each. Tumblers, $7 each. Sugar, $9. Creamer, $9. Vase with flower, $6.

Additional pieces of Forest Green shown at the center are the creamer, $6, the sugar, $6, and the platter, 11", $24.

This was one of my centerpieces for my table at Christmas. The green 13-3/4" sandwich plate in the pattern, "Waterford Waffle" with the green candles in the "Cherokee Rose" candle holders was very attractive. Plate, $13. Candle holders, $70-80.

This was another one of my Christmas center pieces for the table. The deep red 13-1/2" sandwich plate and the candle holders in the pattern "Oyster and Pearl" impressed my guests. In this pattern, there are so many beautiful accessory pieces. The ruby red items are becoming very rare and expensive. I also use these pieces for Valentine's Day. Plate, $45. Candle holders, $50.

WHERE CAN THIS GLASSWARE BE FOUND?

"Garage Sale Today." This is one familiar sign you don't want to pass up. A garage sale is a great place to find pieces of Depression Glass.

Garage sales are gaining in popularity as the sales themselves proliferate all over the country. It is almost impossible to drive in a city on a weekend without seeing a garage sale sign. Signs appear on curbs, front lawns, windows, and doors of houses. Sales are becoming more prevalent in rural areas.

Taking in more than one sale a day is not uncommon for a serious collector. Finding one piece of Depression Glass at one sale excites one about the possibility of finding another at the next.

The local weekly paper lists the various sales, which is an invaluable guide for all collectors. If Depression Glass is listed seek the sale out. Among the miscellaneous items that clutter a table, one can find an elusive and beautiful piece. It is wise to attend all of the sales, because your "find" may be waiting for you at the next stop.

Auctions, gaining in popularity every year, can offer some real "finds" in Depression Glass. Most collectors try buying at auctions. Tales of a complete table setting of pink or cobalt blue Depression Glass or a rare piece of a limited pattern are common. To find these treasures, or just good buys, one must attend numerous auctions, become familiar with the items for sale, and be cautious in bidding. Talking to the owners of the specific items that interest you can be very interesting and rewarding. The actual dates, information, and the true history of these items can be invaluable to any potential bidder, equal to or surpassing the information in a book. The numerous boxes of goodies found at auctions are worth searching through. In some of the boxes there can be the "sleeper," a hard-to-find, long-awaited item among all of the junk. Many have found the exact piece they have been searching for in just this way. The boxes often contain pieces of Depression Glass and sometimes a whole set. Of course every eye would be on this box. One thing to remember about auctions is that the prices for the items purchased are not realistic. The rarity of the piece and the numbers of bidders will determine the actual price. The competition can be very keen. In spite of some of the disadvantages, the auction is a superior source to obtain a variety and a choice of Depression Glass.

Estate sales are another popular source for glassware. The larger cities have more estate sales, and they are sometimes magnificent. Again, like garage sales, early arrival is the key to success in obtaining the choice pieces. There are boxes of numerous items and among them can be choice pieces of elegant glassware. In a way these sales are similar to an auction without the bidding. Some of the estate sales I have attended allow only so many people at a time, or designate numbers for a group to attend. These sales have a variety of beautiful and rare glassware. Never pass up these sales, because more of the elegant glassware often can be found there.

Antique shops are everywhere, and I never tire browsing through them. These are the places where you may find the exact pieces of glassware you are looking for. Some booths have Depression Glass only. Prices of items in these shops may be higher than you anticipate, but whether you can afford it or not, they are a good place for all collectors to become familiar with the various patterns and colors of Depression Glass. The dealers are usually very congenial and eager to share their knowledge with you. This is invaluable to any collector.

Flea markets are becoming very popular all year round. I can attribute much of my collection to them. The dealers there are very eager to sell and willing to compromise on prices. It is at these markets that I have found the mates to my creamers and sugars, the missing cups, bowls and plates to my sets. Most collectors go for these because of the variety and the more reasonable prices. Attending these flea markets can be very rewarding for the novice collector of Depression Glass.

Have you ever visited the thrift shops? They may not seem to appeal to you, but there can be many "steals" there. This is where I found my first pink bon-bon, an uncovered candy dish. The shops are often sponsored by charitable organizations, the Salvation Army, Goodwill, and Saint Vincent de Paul Stores, and offer a variety of glassware of older origin. People bring in items they no longer want, sometimes including complete sets of dishes. I've had great success at these shops finding the missing pieces to my sets of Depression Glass.

New-and-Used stores and consignment shops are another source of collecting. It's amazing what collectibles can be found among the "junk" items. To my surprise, I found a set of glasses to match my favorite Depression Glass pitcher. Consignment shops are good for bargaining.

Attending antique shows is a great way to seek out what you are looking for. There are numerous tables of sparkling Depression Glass of every color and pattern for the collector to view. The interesting part is seeing the complete sets. Talk to the dealers at the shows. They take great pride in their business and can be your best teachers.

The annual church rummage sale is an excellent source for glassware. Searching through all the boxes can be very rewarding and the items are not overpriced. The same is true for clean up drives, annual or semi-annual events where people can set on the curb the things they don't want to be picked up by the city on a certain date, can reveal some special pieces of glassware in boxes or other containers. As I say, "Rummage through trash."

"Silver Crest," Fenton, 1943-present. This is the footed cake plate that is flat with crimped and silver edging. A real "steal" at a garage sale for $3. 13" high, $39.

Garage Sale Finds. Here's a blue opalescent cake plate, flat and footed with numerous hobs, which is a real beauty. Beside the cake plate is the Floragold "Louisa" candy jar and cover in iridescent which was all alone among a bunch of clothes for 75 cents in mint condition. It looked as if it was just waiting for me to take it home. What a "steal" for me as I attended that first sale of the week! In the center is the Waterford "Waffle" crystal, 80 oz. ice lip, tilted pitcher. I had searched a long time for this. Next to the pitcher is the Manhattan, 9-1/2" fruit bowl with the open handles that I had been searching for my set. In front of the bowl was my glorious "find," a blue opalescent crimped bowl for 25 cents. It is "Blossom, No. and Palm," 418 1905, by "Northwood" and signed. When I found it, it was wrapped in old newspaper, very filthy. When cleaned, it was in "mint" condition. **Left to right:** candy jar, $53; cake plate, $40; pitcher, $33; bowl, $36; blue opalescent bowl, crimped, Blossom No. and Palm, Northwood, $85.

Auction Finds. **Left to right:** Iris, "Iris and Herringbone," 9-1/2", footed pitcher, $40; "Starlight," sandwich plate, $15; Cherry Blossom tray, $28; blue vase, $25; and Floragold, "Louisa," a tid-bit with wooden post $32.

Estate Sale Items. **Left:** the Harp, two-handled, rectangular tray, seldom seen, which makes an ideal serving tray and so attractive in the musical design, $33. **Center:** the "Florentine" No. 2, "Poppy No.2," 7-1/2", 28 oz. pitcher, cone-footed. Very dainty with the embossed poppy design on the bottom of the pitcher, $30. **Right:** the "Oyster and Pearl," 13-1/2" sandwich plate, also a liner for the 10-1/2" fruit bowl. Great accessory pieces, $22.

Antique Shops: "Anniversary". **Left to right:** tid-bit berry and fruit bowls with metal handle, $13; plate (standing), round, 12-1/2", $8; "Columbia" butter dish, $20; "Anniversary" candy dish, $22; "Columbia" bowl, 10-1/2", ruffled, $16.

Treasures from Antique Shows and Shops. These are the Waterford, "Waffle" and the Manhattan tray or relish trays, 13-1/2" and 14" with the Manhattan inserts, in red, crystal and pink with the crystal round center insert. These, I put together and use constantly for display or serving purposes. The inserts are becoming difficult to find. Just recently, I found the pink inserts at the Don Wirk Show in Portland, Oregon. The plates I have found at the antique malls. Finding the Manhattan tray complete with the inserts is becoming a challenge. **Left to right:** Waterford "Waffle" with red "Manhattan" and crystal inserts, $44; Waterford "Waffle" with crystal Manhattan inserts, $36; "Manhattan," inserts, and these are pink with crystal insert on the "Manhattan" tray. This is the complete set. $55.

Thrift and Consignment Shops. This is where I found these "Silver Crest" tid-bit, two-tier ruffled plates. What luck!! **Left:** luncheon/dessert, $46. **Right:** luncheon/dinner, $47.

Flea Market finds. Scarce and unusual pieces found in various patterns in crystal, cobalt blue, green, opalescent, and pink. Some real bargains can be found here and the dealers are so willing to make good deals. These are my favorite places to hunt for Depression Glass. I often find the unusual and the missing pieces. **Back row left to right:** Heritage plate, $9; Sandwich tray, $40; Miss America plate, $7; Manhattan vase, $19. **Middle row:** Windsor Diamond pitcher, $13. Sandwich bowl, $7. Waterford "Waffle" salt shaker, $5. Ring, "Banded Ring" tray, $17. Pineapple and Floral bowl, $3. **Front row:** Waterford "Waffle" cups, $5 each; Pretzel bowl, $13; sherbet, cobalt blue, Moderntone, $14; Bowl, green opalescent, $35; Spiral saucer, $3; Bon-bon, $20; Windsor "Windsor Diamond" candlestick, $9.

THE GARAGE SALE ADDICT

With garage sales gaining in popularity all over the country, the addiction to the garage sales is becoming stronger.

It's Wednesday, time for the local weekly shopper to appear in our small town. What am I looking for? Sales advertising glassware, Depression Glass, of course. These sales occur on Thursday, Friday and Saturday. There may be anywhere from 10 to 40 sales. Now it's time to chart my course for the weekly foray. Some look good, and some not so good. Being an avid garage sale shopper, I operate on the principle that you have to attend all of the sales because you never know what you will find.

The time factor is the biggest problem. Most of the sales begin at 8 o'clock in the morning. How can one ever hit them all, and be the first to get at the "cream of the crop"? It is impossible. Some sales stipulate, "No early callers, please," and believe me, that's a life saver.

Some people are knocking on doors at 6 a.m. trying to pick over the sales before they open. Guess it's OK if you don't mind getting up at dawn and if you are lucky enough to get in. A fanatic's brazenness doesn't stop with showing up even the night before. These addicts can be a source of irritation to the

This is an assortment of my garage sale treasures. **In the front** are: the "Floragold, Louisa" candy jar in iridescent, $53; the "Snowflake" 12-3/4" pink cake plate, $30; and the Cameo, "Ballerina" or Dancing Girl 10-1/2" grill plate in yellow, $7. **In the back** are: an 8-9", "Sandwich" bowl in desert gold, $27; Iris, "Iris and Herringbone," 9" iridescent vase, $25; a pink elegant center-handled sandwich plate or tray, $25; a "Moroccan" amethyst candy jar, $32; the pink candy jar of the early Depression Era, $25; and the "Northwood" green opal "Regal" butter dish, $175, toothpick holder, $10, and the spooner, $15.

Left: A pink 9" vase with a round, full bottom of a cubed design with straight vertical lines radiating almost to the top of the flared rim. It was produced in the late 1930s by the Anchor Hocking Glass Company, and was also made in crystal, red, and green. The red and green do not have the flared rim. This is an ideal flower vase, $22. **Right:** an eight-inch "Floral and Diamond Band" berry bowl in green, produced by the U.S. Glass Company, 1927-1931. This green color has a different shade, more of a bluish hue. This is a heavy glass reminiscent of the early pattern glass with sharp cut designs. Searching for the 4-1/2" berry bowls is a challenge. Also came in iridescent and black. $14.

people holding the sale. In search of latent bargains, some buyers ask sellers whether they are willing to sell things that aren't even displayed. Such behavior can be disconcerting to the people holding the sale. These early birds can overwhelm the garage sellers, but this is the typical addict's behavior.

Knowledge of the city is a must for all garage sale addicts. All of the streets and house numbers must be down pat because time is of the essence. Being a ten year veteran of garage sales, I'm quite proficient at spotting garage sales. I prefer to rummage in older neighborhoods where established families have had time to accumulate some stuff worth buying. My eyes are peeled for signs for garage sales that might not have been advertised. They are usually found on telephone poles or light posts. A radio program in my home town, called "Time for Listening," where anyone can call in to advertise their products, the future sales, and auctions, is very helpful and guides one to many good rummage sales. Actually, I have found some real treasures and once in awhile some very rare hidden ones through this advertising media.

The race is on! My first stops are those sales that specify glassware, hopefully Depression Glass. I arise early on a Thursday morning with the list of sales well charted. Pulling up to the first sale, the garage door is shut but cars are lined up on both sides of the street. My friends are there and soon we greet one another and line up on the driveway. All of us try to be the first one by the door. As the door opens, the mad rush is on. Noticing something pink and green on a table in the back part, I rush to that table and quickly grab a vase and bowl. Both items appear to be perfect, and looking quickly and thoroughly at the other items (even in the boxes under the tables), I rush to pay for my goodies. I'm on my way to the next sale. This one reveals no goodies, so I try the next one and continue on until I have covered all of them for the day. I'm very anxious to get home to look over my goodies and determine how valuable they are.

Fridays and Saturdays are the repeat of Thursday. By four o'clock Saturday, the weekly hunt is over. It's time for my Depression Glass friends to call or come over to display and discuss the treasures over a cup of coffee. Most of us are pleased with our goodies. However, there may be a note of envy because one didn't get the goodie the other one got. Sometimes we trade or buy from one another. All in all we rejoice and are happy for one another because this weekly foray did reveal some good treasures.

Not only do I enjoy the sales, but I can't live without seeing one of my addicted garage friends in action in the garage sale jungle. She is working at "junking" as if it is the last act of her life. She pulls up and finds a parking space like it is reserved for her. She knows all the regulars on the garage sale circuit. She darts around town like a bat out of where God doesn't live. Sometimes I question her driving antics, but she makes it safely every time. Being a very religious person she believes that God wants her to have this or that, or that He was saving it for her. Believe me, she knows her stuff and truly personifies the avid garage sale addict.

To the true addict, one garage sale is far from enough. As the saying goes, "Beware! Beware! lest an addict you become." The die hard garage salers can actually take 50 or more sales a week during the heavy season from early spring through early fall.

To find a piece of Depression Glass at a garage sale today takes a truly dedicated person, competing with fellow collectors, waking at the crack of dawn, braving all weather elements, traffic, and being very well informed.

WHY PEOPLE GO TO GARAGE SALES

To some people garage sale rummaging is like window shopping, offering a distraction from the anxiety of life. For many fanatics, hitting the sales seems to fulfill a psychological need. The therapeutic effects of going to garage sales has kept many going after the loss of a loved one, or some other traumatic event in one's life.

Many garage sale rummagers often use their lunch period and dart furiously from sale to sale. To some this is a good, wholesome stimulation to get through the day more quickly. Many garage sale addicts on their way to doctor's appointments or other engagements, are tempted by a garage sale sign and forced to make the difficult choice between stopping or being late for their appointment. Often the stop can calm their anxiety. Even though it is only a brief look, it can reveal a rare treasure. On one stop like this I found a beautiful cake plate in the green "Sunflower" pattern produced by the Jeannette Glass Company in the late 1920s. This three-footed plate with the stylized sunflower

These are the green and pink creamers and sugars that I found after finding the cake plates, $19 each.

This is the green cake plate in the "Sunflower" pattern produced by the Jeannette Glass Company in the late 1920s. This attractive three footed plate with the stylized sunflower in the center surrounded on the border with quite large flowers and foliage was worth my quick stop at the garage sale. This was a premium gift with the purchase of a twenty five pound bag of flour. The pink cake plate was located later, $15 each.

in the center and surrounded on the border with quite large flowers and foliage was worth the quick glance. It was a premium gift with the purchase of a twenty-five pound bag of flour. I also located this cake plate in the pink color and use both of them constantly.

The popularity of garage sales can be attributed to the economic aspect. Many bargains can be found, and shopping for a family can be very economical. Being a garage sale addict myself, I have found many lovely gifts just like new for my family and friends. It is surprising what you can find at these sales. As a result, I have saved a lot of money. Sometimes I think the shopping is more fun than at the mall. As the old saying goes, "One person's junk is another's treasure."

The majority of us are great accumulators. After living in the same house for over thirty years, we have certainly accumulated many, many things. As we have said again and again, we dread the idea of moving. There comes the time, however, when we have to consider the sorting of our accumulation and the disposal of much of it. Having garage sales is the perfect way to get rid of the excess, or as many would say "junk." My sale is among the first of the season's sales, often held on a blustery day in late March. This seems to be a successful time for me. The garage rummager's enthusiasm is the highest after a long, confining winter in Wisconsin. In January, I start to cull out duplicates of Depression Glass and the odd pieces that I can't match or don't need. Among the miscellaneous items I no longer desire to keep can be some great treasures and a "find" for the new or less experienced collector. This has become an annual event and one that my neighbors and friends look forward to. By May the garage season is in full swing.

Garage sales are great meeting places, just like a town square. I dearly love the social aspect, sharing conversation and the treasures with other sale enthusiasts. Relationships develop with the buying, trading, and the selling of the goods. Collecting and selling of Depression Glass has put me in touch with so many interesting people and led to some great friendships. The sales are also good sources of information about upcoming sales and the goodies we might find.

There seems to be something interesting and attractive about other people's possessions and that is perhaps why people like to go to garage sales. In a way it's rather comical to see people nosing around in other's back yards and garages. No, they aren't thieves, just garage sale addicts.

AUCTION FEVER, BEWARE!!

"Auction Today, Follow Arrow." Is this a good place to obtain Depression Glass? Yes. People having the auction have to unload most of the goods they have accumulated over a period of years. This usually involves glassware and especially Depression Glass. If they are an elderly couple, where the glass has passed from generation to generation, the auction will be an excellent source...if you know how to play the auction game.

If you are an amateur beware of the pitfalls.

The first important step is the auction viewing which can be a couple of hours or more before the auction begins. Use the time to scrutinize the Depression Glass very carefully. Searching for glassware requires a good viewing of all the pieces and very close examination. Many of the items can be chipped or badly scratched. It is always wise to have a magnifying glass with you. Never bid on anything unless you have checked it thoroughly. It is not wise to bid on first sight.

Register for a number and choose a good place where you can see what is going on and where the auctioneer can see you. Listen very closely to the bidding which is often extremely fast. Watch out for the regular dealers. They have their own ways of blinking their eyes, nodding their heads, or putting a finger beside their noses to raise their bids. An amateur may end up with some-

This is the Iris, "Iris and Herringbone," 9-1/2", footed iridescent pitcher, produced by the Jeannette Glass Company, 1928-1932; 1950-1970. Very appealing with the unusual, large spray of Iris with its blade like leaves emanating from one point at the inner rim creating a bouquet effect which is very unique and attractive. Very ideal for serving drinks, $40. It is shown with 6", 8 oz. footed tumblers. What an attractive serving set in the iridescent color, match up beautifully with the Iris, "Iris and Herringbone" pitcher. These tumblers are getting harder to find. $19 ea.

thing that he didn't want or couldn't actually afford. Nothing infuriates an auctioneer more than someone who reneges on a bid.

Once you have decided to bid on the glassware you desire, be sure to set your price limit. Once this has been reached, stop. This is the key to successful auction bidding. By abiding in this rule, you'll be able to buy more items and you won't be swept away with the auction fever.

An auction can induce a fever. Everyone seems so fired up and this auction spirit becomes highly contagious. It's sort of a mass hysteria that inflicts the crowd. This auction fever gets everyone in a frenzied mood, losing control, loosening the purse string, and becoming reckless. Just remember to keep the price limit in mind.

When I attend an auction, I focus my eyes on perhaps two or three items, Depression Glass of course, which I examine thoroughly. Then immediately I tell myself these are mine. The feeling of possession takes over. When the time approaches for these items to be auctioned off, I too, get all fired up and auction fever takes over. Breaking my own rule, I sometimes keep bidding regardless of the price limit I have set. When the glass items are in my hands, the joy of ownership is exhilarating. Exceeding the price limit once in awhile is not such a bad habit if the item is rare and in mint condition. Some of my choice pieces of Depression Glass have come from auctions.

The one disadvantage of an auction is the amount of time spent to get the items you want. A whole day can be spent at some auctions, and sometimes in the most uncomfortable conditions. I can recall standing up for hours in 95 degree temperature, acquiring a bad sunburn to get an "Iris and Herringbone" pitcher in the striking iridescent color. Was it worth it? Definitely yes, because I had been searching for this quite awhile and it was in mint condition. The next day I used it, serving lemonade to my guests.

After their first successful bid for many at an auction, many buyers are goners. Some like to hear their number sold over and over again. The auction fever gets higher and tense. The bidders must remember one thing, they have to pay for these items and be satisfied.

Rare items will bring small prices if only one person knows it is rare. Common items will fetch astronomical prices if two people keep each other from owning it. Dealer lists and auction results are the two worst indicators of true prices.

People go to auctions for the same reason they go to rummage sales: to seek bargains. Need is not what auctions are all about, it is just the "steals" you can get. Besides that, an auction is a great social event and many friendships have been formed. Collectors enjoy seeing the same people at auction after auction. One can also experience the nostalgia of the past with the display of the old items, yesterday's treasures.

Auction's are fun, even enjoying the musical auctioneer's cry. In the boxes of various, sometimes quite junky items, like plastic and old chipped plates, can be discovered a very old, very valuable item nestled in a corner. The surprise and joy of finding these unexpected treasures keep people coming back.

THE STRIKING ARRAY OF COLORS

These were the principal Depression Era colors that were the rage throughout the country. First, it was pink, deep amethyst, bright ruby, spring green, darker green, white, opalescent, light blue, cobalt blue, royal blue, canary, primrose yellow, amber luster, topaz, iridescent, black and crystal. **Back row left to right:** vase, Moonstone, $12; pitcher, Depression, $25; pitcher, amethyst, $30; tumbler, forest green, $5; pitcher, Royal ruby, $30. **Middle row left to right:** sugar, Cameo, yellow, $19; Twisted Optic preserve with slotted lid, $30; bowl, cobalt blue with gold, $20; pitcher, Aurora, cobalt blue, $22; bowl with ladle, topaz, $20. **Front row left to right:** iridescent "Bubble" bowl, amber,$4; sherbet, Iris, "Iris and Herringbone," $15; bowl, Cubist crystal, $8; bowl, Swirl, $15; sugar and creamer, Vitrock, $4 each; sugar, Mt. Pleasant, black, $15; bowl, Fire-King, 1-pint, turquoise blue; $13.

Color was bursting out everywhere in the Depression Era. Everyone appreciated color in America and the rage for colored glass swept wildly throughout the country. If anything could alleviate the drabness of the Depression it was color.

Color was very fashionable in glassware. The principal Depression Era colors were pink, deep amethyst, bright ruby, spring green, darker green, white, opalescent, light blue, cobalt blue, royal blue, canary, primrose yellow, amber lustre, topaz, iridescent, black, and crystal.

Pink was the popular color in the early 1920s and is still the popular color among collectors in the 1990s. Whenever a piece of pink glass appears at a garage sale it seems to attract attention from everyone. Sometimes the competition to obtain these pieces is extreme. Pink is becoming more elusive daily. It is a very interesting and impressive color.

The first pink was called Rose and was the principal color in the 1920s. The year 1926 was a good year for rose pink. One company called their pink "Roselin" in 1926, while others named it Dawn, Rose Lustre and Nurose. Flamingo and Cerise were other names for the color pink until the color was discounted in 1942. Pink was the sensation at the Pittsburgh glass exhibit and others, as well as in the homes of America during this era.

Green, so fresh and bright and vibrant looking, is the typical Depression color. This color, too, had various names, including Emerald, Springtime Green, Forest Green, Imperial Green, Jade, Chartreuse and Opaque Jade Green. In 1931, jade, a soft whitish-green was introduced along with the black-midnight combination. Jadite, opaque jade green, was popular in 1932. Evergreen, a dark green, made its debut in 1931. Chartreuse, a unique yellow green, very soft color, was produced in 1948. Ultra marine, a dark blue-green color, was the popular color in 1937 and 1938. Jade green is a generic name used by many companies. The Anchor Hocking Company produced a lot of the green glassware. Many of the kitchen accessories were made in green - so fresh looking in the kitchen.

Cobalt blue, a color with the mystique all of its own, was produced in limited quantities and this accounts for its rarity. It is a strong, rich color and is in strong demand by all collectors. This color was sometimes called Ritz Blue, Dark Blue and Deep Blue. Ritz Blue made its debut in 1936.

Amber, a brownish-yellow color with different shades, became very popular in accessories items by Depression Glass devotees.

In the 1930s, black was introduced. Sometimes it came decorated with gold, a white band, or silver trim. Black is black opaque glass and was extremely popular all through the 1930s. It was produced in limited quantities by L.E. Smith Company. Black is great for accessories, adding a sharp accent with the other colors of glassware on tables, mantels, shelves and in hutches. Depression glass collectors seek out all of the black that can be found.

Much Delfite glassware, a soft blue opaque color popular in table settings, was made by the Jeannette Company. Jeannette's Junior Dinner Set was a great hit in this color.

Amethyst, a very rich, purplish tint, was popular in the 1920s and 1930s. This color usually attracts the collectors in any pattern, and is rarer than cobalt blue. "Moroccan" in amethyst is an extremely attractive dinnerware set. Burgundy, also a purplish tint nearly the same as amethyst, was very popular with the Hazel Atlas Company and many beautiful pieces were made.

Cremex, a creamish color, Turene, an ivory color, and Monax, opaque white, were popular colors used by Macbeth-Evans. Beautiful and complete sets of dinnerware can be found in these colors.

Short runs of other colors like amberina, ambrosa, ocean blue and florentine green were made throughout the years.

Satin finish is treated glassware rather than a color applied to a transparent glass. The special acid-etching results in a cloudy or frosted appearance. Collector's reactions to this type of glassware are mixed.

There can be a difference in the shades of all these colors, lighter and darker. Royal Ruby by Hocking is different from the ruby red of another company's patterns.

Color helped to conceal the impurities and minute flaws in the glassware. As you examine some of the pieces you will notice that the color is deepest where the glass is thicker. This gives the glassware its special appeal.

Few people realize what a great role color played in this era. Advertising emphasized the glamour of serving the food in colored glassware. With the emphasis on color so strong, the rainbow of vibrant colors is something to behold. For twenty years these colors retained their popularity.

In 1935 the trend back to crystal, or clear glass, began. Color was combined with crystal to interesting effect.

Today there is renewed interest in the popularity of these colors, with many companies reproducing the popular patterns. Pink is the one color that seems to retain its popularity.

Back row left to right: Miss America by Hocking Glass Co. 1935-1938. Bowl, curved in top in a strong deep rose luster with the hobnail motif and large sunburst of radial lines. 8", $72; pitcher, 80 oz., in Rose Glow, by the Federal Glass Co. in the early 1920s and 1930s, $25; candy dish, in rose pink, produced by Imperial Co., 1925-1935. 5-1/4", $20. **Front row left to right:** "Doric" creamer and sugar in light pink. This is a classical pattern with a small star in the center, surrounded by four motifs of four loops each. Twelve lines radiate to a border of twelve miniature panels. Produced by the Jeannette Glass Co., 1935-1938. Creamer, $10. Sugar and lid, $14; cupped fruit bowl in the color Nu-Rose, center handle, produced by Bartlett Collins Co. in Sapulpa, Oklahoma in 1927. 10", $35; candlestick, in a strong deep rose luster, in the elegant glassware line, $10.

Sharon, "Cabbage Rose," Federal Glass Company, 1935-1939. A very popular chipped mold dinnerware pattern. Plates have an off-center motif of a curved spray of cabbage roses and spokes on border. The scarcest item is the covered cheese dish. **Left to right:** creamer, $18; sugar, $15; platter, $30; cream soup, $42; butter dish and cover, $47.

Green was the typical Depression Glass color. This color took on variations and companies had specific names for the green. **Left to right:** creamer and sugar set, $10; Sharon, "Cabbage Rose" sugar. A brighter and darker green, $16; forest green pitcher, $22. A popular color produced by the Anchor Hocking Glass Co. in 1950-1967; Nu green stemware goblets, vertical lines by Bartlett Collins from 1927-1930s, 7-1/4", $10; flower bowl, console in Nu green popular in the 1920s, $20; Floral and Diamond Band Bowl, $14. This has a bluish green color; Twisted Optic preserve and cover, $30. A bright green color, $30; Swirl, "Petal Swirl" sugar and creamer, dark blue-green color, ultra-marine, $14 each.

Fire King Jade-ite, Jane Ray Anchor Hocking Co. 1945-1960s. The jade, a soft whitish-green, was introduced with the black-midnight combination. Jadite an opaque jade green was very popular in 1932. Kitchen accessories were in this popular color. **Clockwise from the left:** cup and saucer, $4; dinner plate, 9-1/8", $8; cereal bowl, 5-7/8", $6; egg cup, $7.

The black color became popular in the mid-1920s, by L. E. Smith Co. Tableware and novelties were popular. Here are black pieces in combination with the Jade-ite seen in the previous photograph. Left: Egg cup on black pedestal, $10. Bowl on black pedestal, $11.

Cobalt Blue. This is the strong, rich blue color with a mystique all of its own. Due to limited quantities it is very scarce and expensive. **Left to right:** vase, $5; mustard dish without the metal cover in the pattern of Petalware, by Macbeth-Evans Glass Co. 1930-1940, $6; tumbler, Georgian by Fenton Art Co. in 1930, $8; vase with flared top, $10; toothpick holder, Cobalt blue, decorated on the indented sides like a star, $5; swan, cobalt blue of the Depression Glass era. Made of melted down glass from bottles and other glassware. This swan is identified as a six point and 11-1/2", $40; violin, cobalt blue with side tabs at the neck. This bottle is of the figural type, ABM. 8" high, $25; sherbet, Moderntone, "Wedding Band," Cobalt blue, $14; tilt pitcher, cobalt blue, 32 oz., ice-lipped. This fine ribbed resembles the Homespun pattern, $35; creamer, Moderntone, "Wedding Band" Hazel Atlas Co. 1934-1942. Typifies the decorative are style of the 1930s, with the widely spaced concentric rings. Cobalt blue, $12.

Amber. Left: console fruit bowl, Diana, Federal Glass Co. 1937-1941. Made by pressed-mold method and manufactured for a few years. This is a very simple pattern of fine swirled radial lines leading out from the center of the plates with wide rims of slightly larger curved lines, 11", $15. **Right:** console bowl, Sandwich Anchor Hocking Glass Co. 1939-1964. Amber (desert gold). Traditional American pattern in pressed glass. Has all-over stippling spaced around flower, foliage, and scroll motifs in elaborate arrangement. 9", $27. **Center:** platter, "Daisy", 620 Indiana Glass Co., late 1930s. This pattern, in amber, is becoming very popular in the mid-west. The arrangement of daisies around the border of the pieces make this set very attractive. 10-3/4", $14.

Black. Introduced in the 1930s, black became very popular. It came decorated with gold, white, silver, pink, and added a sharp accent. This color is scarce due to production of limited quantities. The L.E. Smith Company produced a lot of this, with a rich, striking color, and any piece can be displayed with great pride. **Back row, left and right:** compote, Saw Tooth (Mitre Diamond). Fenton and U.S. Glass Companies produced this line of glassware. Covered compote, $42 each. **Back center:** Plate, decorated, $10. Covered compote, $42. **Front row, left to right:** vase, ruffled, $8; rose bowl, footed with crystal frog, $12; sandwich plate, center-handled tray, black, gold and pink, $25; sugar, Mt. Pleasant, $15; saucer, Ouide, $2; candlesticks, "Mt. Pleasant," $25 pr.

Amethyst. This is a very rich purplish color and very popular with collectors. It is quite scarce, more so than cobalt blue. "Moroccan" in amethyst and "Moderntone" are two beautiful dinnerware sets. **Left to right:** saucer, $1; vase, $8; plate, $9; swan, $20; compote, $10; cup, $5.

Console bowl with wings,
on pedestal (round), 13",
$40.

Chip and dip bowls in a metal holder. 10-3/4" & 5-3/4". Pattern, Moroccan Amethyst, $37.
12" plate, $10.

Satinized compote, blue decorated, and a
ruffled top, $12. Satinized finish has not
been too popular with collectors.

Cremex, Ivory and Monax. **Back left:** Luncheon plate, American Sweetheart, Macbeth Evans Glass Co. 1930-1936, in Monax. 9", $9. This is one of the most popular of any of the Macbeth Evans patterns. Mold-etched and made in a great variety of colors than most depression colors. Has a neat arrangement of a center motif of festoons, ribbons and scroll designs with smaller surrounding the scalloped rim. It has 10 short radial lines to the border. **Back center:** Petalware, Macbeth Evans Glass Co. 1930-1940. A very versatile design, some having hand applied colored bands and simple floral motifs with fluted rims and scalloped edges. Sandwich Plate or Salver, 11", $11. **Back right:** Plate in ivory, 9-3/4", $4. Chinex Classic, Macbeth Evans Division of Corning Glass Works, late 1930s-early 1940s. This pattern is gaining popularity, but becoming scarce. It has an embossed, scroll-like design in the dishes which distinguishes them from Cremex which can be confusing to collectors. **Cups and saucers, left to right:** Cup and saucer (Ivory, Chinex Classic), $6; Cup and saucer (Monax), $12; Cup and saucer, (Cremax, decorated), $5. **Front right:** Vegetable bowl, 9", $7. This is called Cremex, Macbeth Evans Division of Corning Glass Works, late 1930s-early 1940s. Floral decals are found on this pattern. Cremax was used to describe the beige-like color.

An art deco type of satinized decorated bowl and plate. This is a very attractive set. Produced in the 1930s and 1940s. Bowl, three footed, 11-1/2", $30. Plate, footed, 13-1/2", $20.

Crystal. In 1935 the trend to the return of crystal took effect. The clear glass was called crystal by all of the glass companies.

Left: large Waterford, "Waffle" berry bowl, 8-1/4", $10. Hocking Glass Company 1938-1944. A distinctive pattern with the radial sunburst lines, triple concentric circle of small blocks and the rim with a lattice or waffle design. **Center:** glass basket. An elegant type, footed with a beaded design. Initials of DB on the sides of the handle. Very heavy and attractive. 11-1/2" wide, $125. **Right:** pretzel, berry bowl. Produced by Indiana Glass Company, late 1930-1980s. This is a unique pattern consisting of crossed or x-shaped ribs. The fruit pattern, plain or colored is more difficult to find and more expensive in the center of the plates. 9-3/8", $17.

Back: glass basket from previous photograph, $125. **Front left:** bowl, round divided, two-handled. Candlewick Line #400 Imperial Glass Company 1936-1984, 6", $25. **Front center:** bowl, heart-shaped. This is an elegant glassware produced in a big line. Very attractive with the beaded effect. Some pieces are hard to find. 5-1/2", $15. **Front right:** Crystolite tray, Blank #1503. A.H. Heisey and Company. This is another pattern in the elegant glassware. This is very attractive with the large ribbed and beaded effect. Some pieces are difficult to find. 12", 3 pt. relish, $30.

INTRIGUING PATTERNS
OF DEPRESSION GLASS

What pattern is this beautiful pink or green plate? This is the common question when we acquire the first piece of glassware. This piece of glassware with the circles, spirals, swirls, depressed dots, horizontal and vertical ribbed lines, block shapes, floral designs and fruit motifs constitutes the most attractive, elaborate and fascinating patterns ever produced in glassware.

The names reflect geography, religion, history, geometric, nature, romance, patriotism, people, music, elegance and special events.

Geographical names include Madrid, Florentine, Normandie, Aurora, Columbia, Newport and Manhattan.

Adam, with its intricate and lavish display of leaves, flowers, and scrolls resembling ferns, creates a garden type scene as in the biblical story.

The historical names are American Pioneer, Old English, Lincoln Inn, Vernon, Queen Mary, Windsor and Coronation (so aristocratic and British sounding).

In the geometric category there are the names Colonial Block, Hexoptic, Sierra Pinwheel, Circle, Spiral, Cubist, Pretzel, Twisted Optic, Swirl, Ring Banded Ring, Ribbon, and Horseshoe.

Flower names include Sharon Cabbage Rose, Orchid, Sunflower, Poinsetta, Stippled Rose, Mayfair Open Rose, Cherry Blossom, Cherokee Rose, Daisy, Rose Cameo, Rosemary Dutch Rose, and Cloverleaf. Also in the nature category are the bird related names like Nora Bird, Round Robin, Peacock Reverse, Georgian Lovebirds and Parrot Sylvan. The names of fruits, Pineapple, Strawberry and Avocado are nature related too.

In the romantic theme are the names American Sweetheart, Starlight, Moonstone, Moondrops, Moderntone Wedding Band, Radiance, Princess and Diamond Quilted.

Miss America, a very popular favorite of mine with the hobnail motif was named to appeal to American patriotism. Victory, an art deco design with its unique variety and quality glassware fits into this patriotic category.

People's names in the patterns include Aunt Polly, Diana, Roxanna and Lorraine.

Harp, a name reflecting its musical design attracts collector after collector. The big attraction in this pattern are the variety of the magnificent cake stands. To find them all is a real challenge for the collector.

The elegant names in the patterns are Waterford, Laced Edge, Lace Edge Open Lace, Chinex Classic, Royal Lace, Rock Crystal and Oyster and Pearl.

Special event names are Holiday, Anniversary and Jubilee.

Knowing the proper name of the pattern is the key to collecting. The knowledge of the various patterns is extremely essential for the collector in identifying the glass pattern and manufacturer with the date.

An excellent way to become familiar with the patterns is to gather examples of as many as you can find and then research them.

It is very interesting and challenging to watch the pieces of the many patterns fall into place. So many of the items are on the elusive list. Many collectors are now picking up as much as they can find because some of the patterns are reaching the "endangered species" level.

Some of the patterns were used extensively and therefore the pieces can be badly scratched and damaged. Some were more vulnerable to chips and breakage like Sierra, "Pinwheel" by Jeannette Glass Company with its impractical serrated edges. Manhattan, "Horizontal Ribbed", by Anchor Hocking Glass Company with the sharp ribbing can chip easily if not handled carefully, but is a real collector item. Old Colony "Lace Edge," "Open Lace," also by Hocking Glass Company has the pierced, or open border design which is prone to chipping. This is an elegant pattern of a beautiful pressed design. Tea Room by Indiana Glass Company with its extreme art deco style is another pattern quite vulnerable to chipping. Tea Room reflects the decorative art style of the 1920s and 1930s. This was an early pattern, extreme in style, being heavily pressed, geometric, and in flashy shapes. This pattern was made for restaurants and soda fountains in thirty different shapes. The banana-split boat appeals to today's nostalgia buffs.

New collectors respond to some of the simpler patterns as they are easier for the novice collector to identify.

For beginning collectors, Heritage, a beautiful, striking crystal in hobs is a very wise choice. It's a small pattern, quite available and relatively inexpensive. Because it has fewer types, this set is easier to assemble. Heritage is gaining in popularity and becoming a favorite among young collectors. Bubble by Anchor Hocking seems to infatuate new collectors. In crystal this glassware is priced fairly cheap due to availability. Crystal Bubble makes a very attractive looking table and is picking up in popularity. The blue Bubble is a favorite of mine and I use this for special occasions like anniversary and birthday dinners. It makes an attractive setting any day. Amber Bubble is very appealing but scarce, as it was short lived or experimental. This factor also applies to many other patterns.

Royal Ruby seems to put a gleam in the collector's eye, and when it appears on the market it is grabbed up very quickly. This is very festive and rich pattern good for Christmas, as is Forest Green.

Many of the patterns typify the decorative art style of the 1930s. Pyramid by Indiana Glass Company is a heavy art deco type of glass. It is becoming extremely popular, but it is scarce. When purchasing this, be careful to check all of the angles, sides, and edges. With the protruding points this pattern is very vulnerable to chipping. Starlight and Sierra Pinwheel are of the art deco style.

Some patterns are so popular that they are called "Stars." These include Cameo, Cherry Blossom, Mayfair, Miss America, Sharon, "Cabbage Rose," Manhattan, Iris, and "Iris and Herringbone."

Thumbprint is one of the oldest Depression Era patterns. It appeared even before the mold-etched designs. Spiral is another with swirled lines in a pinwheel effect.

Everyone seems to have a favorite pattern and that helps the collector to obtain all of the pieces for the complete setting.

There are some patterns that command high prices like Georgian Lovebirds and Parrot, the kingpin of Depression Glass. These have doubled in popularity in recent years. Jubilee, with its scarcity, continues to rise in price. Iris, "Iris and Herringbone", extremely popular, has increased significantly in price.

Treasured patterns like Princess, Royal Lace, Laced Edge and Lace Edge Open Lace are garnered by many a collector for their mold-etched, decorative and elaborate designs. The mold-etching so distinctive of Depression Glass is very representative of the time.

Some patterns have had tremendous longevity. English Hobnail is one of these.

Seek out all of the patterns as some of them have been overlooked for their potentiality. Oyster and Pearl, a short-lived pattern, is a very attractive pattern and is ideal for gift items and accessories.

Similarities in patterns will be easier to recognize with knowledge and thorough viewing. There are numerous swirled and spiraled patterns.

What is interesting are the unusual variety of forms found in some of the patterns. These include a boat-shaped vegetable bowl, a hat-shaped fruit bowl, a banana boat split, cone-shaped pitchers, a block butter dish, tilt jug and pitchers, fish bowl cookie jar, vase, hat-shaped, heart-shaped jelly dish, a hexagonal cookie jar, octagonal salad bowl, club, diamond, heart and spade ash trays and V-shaped creamer, sugar and sherbets.

The table settings in the 1930s were something to be admired. The style was to set the table in a single pattern and color with every piece matching and serving a purpose. This coordinated table setting served the family meal, the shining center in their lives together.

Today we set our tables in a hurry with unmatching pieces of dishes and sometimes with disposable paper cups and plates. Often times our dinners are the prepared TV dinners served on a TV tray and shared with the television set. The era of gracious living seems to have vanished with society becoming more fast paced and complex.

All of these various shapes from the circle to the diamond shape make this glassware so unique and fascinating. **Left to right:** Circle sherbet, $5; Spiral sherbet, $5; Swirl bowl, $15; dot tumbler, $7; horizontal, Manhattan bowl, $18; vertical, Queen Mary creamer, $8; Block saucer, $2; Daisy tumbler, $18; Pineapple floral comport, $1.

Pattern names reflect interests in geography, religion, history, geometric, nature, romance, patriotism, people, music, elegance and special events. It is interesting how these names were selected for the patterns. One of the men working at the Federal Glass plant named the "Diana" pattern after his daughter. These are some of the geographical names. **Left to right:** Madrid sherbet, $8; Florentine no. 1 cup, $9; Normandie plate, $8; Aurora pitcher, $22; Columbia butter dish, $20; Newport creamer, $13; Manhattan comport, pink, 5-3/4", $33.

The Adam pattern, after a biblical figure. **Left to right:** candy jar & cover, $85; saucer, $6; sherbet plate, $6; dessert bowl, $14; berry bowl, 9", $25; dessert bowl, $14.

Historical names. **Left to right:** Coronation, "Banded-Rib," rib bowls, 8" ($16), 6-1/2" ($12), 4-1/4" ($6); Queen Mary, plate ($5), celery dish ($10), sherbet ($4), salt & pepper, $19 pr.; Coronation Pink, sherbet ($5), bowl ($9), cup ($5).

Geometric names. **Left to right:** Circle sherbet, $5; Hex Optic tumbler, $4; Block sugar, $12; Swirl bowl, $15; Pretzel plate, $14; Cubist creamer, $2; Ring, Banded Ring creamer, $5; Horse Shoe plate, $12; Twisted Optic (similar to) Candlestick, $8; Twisted Optic preserve, $30.

Floral names. **Left to right:** Cherokee Rose candlestick, $35; Rose Cameo tumbler, $22; Cherry Blossom tray, $28; Daisy cup & saucer, $9; Mayfair goblet, $58; Rosemary "Dutch Rose" plate, $5; Poinsettia bowl with cover, $30.

Floral nature names. **Left to right:** Sharon, "Cabbage Rose" creamer, $18, sugar, $15; "S" pattern, "Stippled Rose Band" creamer, $6, plate, $10, sugar, $6; Sunflower sugar, $19; creamer, $19. **Front center:** Mayfair relish, $25.

Among the favorite patterns with a nature name is Georgian, "Love Birds" Federal Glass Company, 1931-1936. Creamer, $14. Sugar, $15.

Fruit names. **Front, left to right:** No. 618, "Pineapple & Floral," Indiana Glass Company, 1932-1937. Salad bowl, 7", $3; relish platter, 11-1/2", $18; sugar, $7; creamer (diamond shaped), $7. **Back:** Milk glass plate, Westmoreland Glass Co., late 1930s-1950s, "Beaded edge," 10-1/2", $30.

Romantic names. **Back left:** "American Sweetheart" plate, $25. **Back right:** "Princess" grill plate, $14. **Front, left to right:** "Starlight" bowl 8-1/2", $11; "Diamond Quilted" bowl, $7; "Moderntone" plate, $12; "Moonstone" candy jar & cover, $25.

Among patriotic names, Miss America is a favorite. **Left to right:** platter, $15; saucers, $3; grill plate, 10-1/4", $10; bowl, 8", $72; plate, 8-1/2", $7; sugar, $9; creamer, $9.

People's names. **Left:** Diana, bowl, scalloped, 12", $8; sandwich plate, 11-3/4", $7. **Right:** Loraine Basket no. 615, platter, yellow, 11-1/2", $43; sherbet-yellow footed, $31.

Harp is a beautiful pattern with a musical name. **Back row left to right:** plate, crystal, 7", $12; cake stand, 9", $22; plate 7", $12. **Front row:** ashtray/coasters, $5; coasters, $5.

Elegant names. **Front left:** Oyster and Pearl relish dish, oblong, divided, 10-1/4", $11. **Back left:** Rock Crystal relish bowl, six-part, 14", $38. **Center:** Chinex Classic cup & saucer, $6. **Back right:** Waterford Waffle plate, 9-3/8", $11. Right: Old Colony, "Lace Edge" open lace flower bowl, $27.

Special names. **Left:** Jubilee. Creamer, $23; sugar, $23. **Center:** Anniversary. Candy jar & cover, $22. **Right:** Holiday, Buttons & Bows. Creamer, footed, $8.

These are some of the pieces that are becoming very difficult to find. Much searching is needed to find these pieces to complete the patterns. Cereal bowls, sherbets, tumblers and dinner plates are becoming more scarce. Among the scarce items are:

>Waterford "Waffle" - cereal bowls and tumblers.
>"Old Cafe" and "Forest Green" dinner plates.
>"Starlight" sherbets.
>"Bubble" creamer.
>"Heritage" creamer and sugar.

Left to right: bowl, Cherry Blossom, two-handled, 9", $45; pitcher, Florentine, "Poppy no. 2" cone footed, yellow. 28 oz. 7-1/2", $30; creamer, "Bubble," blue, $35; Royal Ruby plate, 13-3/4", $35; tumbler, "Bow Knot," 10 oz., footed, 5", $12; cereal bowl, Waterford, "Waffle," 5-1/2", $18; sherbet, Starlight crystal, $14; Tumbler, Waterford "Waffle," 10 oz., footed, 4-7/8", $15; dinner plate, Old Cafe, 10", $35; cereal bowl, Starlight, closed handles, 5-1/2", $10; Royal Ruby salad bowl, 11-1/2", $32.

Heritage, Federal Glass Company 1940-1955. A very attractive pattern becoming very popular with collectors today. It is quite available except for the creamer and sugar, which are challenges. **Back row left to right:** luncheon plate, 8", $9; sandwich plate, 12", $14; dinner plate, 9-1/4", $12. **Front row left to right:** berry bowl, 5", $9; cup, $7; fruit bowl, 10-1/2", $15; saucer, $4; large berry bowl, 8-1/2", $36.

Bubble, "Bullseye" Provincial, Anchor Hocking Glass Company crystal, 1940-1965. This is another pattern that is easy for all collectors to identify, and quite available, except for some pieces, the blue creamer, and the 9" flanged bowl in blue. Plates and bowls have the scalloped edges, centers with a radial sunburst ending in a circle of bull's eye dots. **Front left to right:** sugar, $5; creamer, $5; cup-saucer, $5; soup bowl, 7-3/4", $7; plate, 6-3/4", $3; bowl, 4-1/2", $4; bowl, 5-1/4", $5. **Back:** platter, oval, 12", $8; dinner plate, 9-3/8", $6.

Bubble (blue). This is a very popular pattern and makes an attractive dinner pattern. **Back left:** plate, 9-3/8", $8. **Back right:** platter, 12", $18. **Front, left to right:** sugar, $20; creamer, $35; bowl, flat, 7-3/8", $15; fruit bowl, 4-1/2", $12; berry bowl, 8-3/8", $16; cup and saucer, $11; plate, 6-3/4", $4; candlesticks, crystal, $16 pr.

Red (iridescent) and green are increasing in popularity. **Left:** Bubble Royal Ruby, tumbler, 8 oz., $10; tumbler, 12 oz., $12; pitcher, $50. **Center left:** Bubble Iridescent, bowl, 8-3/8", $12; bowl, 4", $4. **Center right:** Bubble Pink, bowl, 8-3/8", $9. **Right:** Bubble Green, creamer, $11; sugar, $11.

Several patterns have become known as the "stars" because of their popularity. They include:

Miss America (diamond patter) Hocking Glass Co. 1943-1938.

Cameo, "Ballerina" or Dancing Girl Hocking Glass Co. 1930-1934, the only pattern in Depression Glass that has a human figure as part of the decoration. Little dancing girls with long draped scarves appear in the borders of the plates and are surrounded by festoons and ribbon rows.

Manhattan, "Horizontal Wide Ribbed," Anchor Hocking Glass 1938-1943. This pattern is in contrast to Hocking's more traditional shapes and patterns. Very attractive in pink.

Sharon "Cabbage Rose," Federal Glass Company, 1935-1939. This is very popular dinnerware in pink. Plates have an off-center motif of a curved spray of cabbage roses with spokes on border. The scarcest item is the covered cheese dish.

Mayfair, "Open Rose," Hocking Glass Company 1931-1937. This pattern has a center circle of roses, widely spaced lines, square plates have a border of roses and scalloped.

Iris, "Iris and Herringbone," Jeannette Glass Co. 1928-1932; 1950-1970. This is a highly collectible pattern in spite of its reproduction. It has an unusual, large spray of iris flowers with the blade-like leaves emanating from one point at the outer rim, creating a bouquet effect. Unique and attractive.

"Star" Patterns. **Front, left to right:** Miss America relish plate, four-part, pink. 8-3/4", $25; Manhattan bowl, 4-1/2", $9; Mayfair, deep scalloped fruit bowl, loop handles, 12" deep, $56; Iris, "Iris and Herringbone" vase, iridescent, 9", $25. **Back, left to right:** Cameo, "Ballerina" or "Dancing Girl," grill plate, 10-1/2", $7; Sharon Cabbage Rose, platter, oval, 12-1/2", $30; Cherry Blossom, sandwich tray, open handles, 10-1/2", $28.

Some patterns are extremely popular, but becoming scarce and expensive.

Georgian "Lovebirds," Federal Glass Co. 1931-1936. The motif of birds in pairs and the baskets in the border of the plates give this pattern a subdued classical appearance.

Jubilee, Lancaster Glass Company, early 1930s. This is highly sought after and expensive glassware.

Iris. Iris and Herringbone, Jeannette Glass Co., 1928-1950. A popular pattern in crystal and iridescent, in great demand by all collectors.

Left to right: Georgian Lovebirds, sugar, $15; creamer, $14; Iris, "Iris and Herringbone" sauce bowl, 5-1/2", $20; Jubilee, plate 8-3/4", $16; sherbet, 8 oz., 3", $70; "Iris and Herringbone" tumbler, 6", $19; sherbet, $15.

There are some especially treasured patterns.

Old Colony, "Lace Edge," Open Lace, Hocking Glass Co. 1936-1938, is the only pressed pattern of this type with a pierced or open border design. Well known pattern among veteran depression glass collectors.

Princess, Hocking Glass Company. 1931-1935, is attractive with the octagonal shape, the center motif snowflake.

Left to right: relish plate, three-part, 10-1/2", $25; "Princess," cake plate, 10", $20; hat-shaped bowl, 9-1/2", $42.

Oyster and Pearl Accessories. **Left to right:** candlesticks, $22 pr.; bowls, heart-shaped, one-handle, crystal or pink, 5-1/4", $8; sandwich plate, 13-1/2", $18; deep fruit bowl, 10-1/2", $22.

The variety of shapes is what makes Depression Glass so interesting to collect. **Left to right:** butter dish, square crisscross, $18; Old Colony cookie jar (without cover), "Lace Edge," $30; banana split bowl, $6. "Windsor Diamond" bowl, boat shape, 7"x 11-3/4", $34; Sandwich glass ashtrays, $3 each; Oyster & Pearl, serving nappie, 5-1/2", $8; Royal Ruby, tilt pitcher, 3-quart, $40; banana split boat, $6; Newport, sugar, $7, creamer, v-shaped, $7.

"MOONSTONE"

It was exceedingly difficult for me to choose my favorite pattern when I am totally charmed with every pattern and color of Depression Glass. However, the one big sandwich plate that I inherited from my mother very definitely caught my eye with its brilliant sparkle and opalescent color then and it still does now.

This is striking crystal glassware which features opalescent trim on the rims and hobnails. It was produced by the Anchor Hocking Glass Corporation from 1941 to 1946.

Opalescent is glass that resembles an opal in color, usually bluish white and translucent unless held to a strong light when it will show red highlights. Opalescent glass was first produced in 1897 in America at the Northwood Glassworks in Indiana, Pennsylvania. It is sometimes called "opaline" and opalescent mainly for its translucence.

Moonstone Display. This is the striking crystal with the opalescent hobnails. This pattern attracts all collectors for its variety of novel pieces. The goblets are becoming scarce. **Back row left to right:** divided relish bowl, 7-3/4", $11; bud vase, 5-1/2", $12; sandwich plate, 10-3/4", $26; luncheon plate, 8-3/8", $15; goblet, 10 oz., $19. **Middle row left to right:** creamer, $8; sugar, $9; cup & saucer, $15; sherbet, $7; crimped bowl, 9-1/2", $20; flat bowl, 7-3/4", $12; handled bowl, crimped, 6-1/2", $9. **Front row left to right:** heart shaped bon-bon, one handle, $12; berry bowl, flat (scarce), 5-1/2", $16; clover leaf bowl, $12. puff box and cover, round, 4-3/4", $22; crimped dessert bowl, 5-1/2", $9.

Other Opalescent Pieces. The pieces are fun to search for and can be added to the Moonstone set. Fenton produced numerous pieces like this. **Back row left to right:** vase, $8; candle holder, $8. **Front row left to right:** candle holder, $5; sugar 2", $6; mustard dish, with ladle, 2", $10; creamer, 2", $6; candle holder, $5.

For beginning collectors it is significant to distinguish the opalescent items made by the Fenton Glass Company. The Fenton Company has been long known for its opalescent hobnail and has produced many items like pitchers, tumblers, shakers, vases, nappies and some novel items. One distinguishing factor is the hobs which are more pointed than the round hobs on the Moonstone pattern by Anchor Hocking. Another way to distinguish the Moonstone from the Fenton products is the many-rayed star relief in the center and on the feet of most items. The Fenton, Duncan and Miller Company's products do not have this rayed effect.

All of the Fenton items can be added to your Moonstone set and will match quite well as the color is so similar. Many collectors are now doing this and I am, too, because I love the opalescent color. All of these additions enhance the beauty of my set. The cologne bottle which is commonly seen among the Moonstone display is a Fenton product. This is a very unique addition to my set and a novel item in the collection.

The luncheon sets were given as gifts during World War II. These sets were extremely popular and are ideal for serving luncheons.

As my favorite, I have collected every piece of this pattern being fortunate in finding the 5-1/2" uncrimped berry bowls which are becoming scarce and the prices escalating. I would suggest that beginning collectors pick up anything they find in Moonstone as it will be less and less available. This pattern is a good seller and dealers don't keep it long in their shops.

I enjoy displaying my Moonstone. It is especially impressive on a blue, pink, and green background. The candlesticks are fun to work with for display with the various colored candles. This set is put to good use and I enjoy it immensely. For luncheons it is my favorite and a great conversation piece among the guests.

Moonstone makes a very striking overall table setting with the bluish-white effect. When I use this set for birthday, anniversary and other special events, my guests describe it as "impressive."

Moonstone seems to be the eye catcher for anyone who comes into my home. For many it has become their favorite, too.

Luncheon Set. The basic four-piece luncheon set, consisting of a bowl, a luncheon plate, a cup, and a saucer, was given away as a promotional gift. This set is very attractive and ideal for any luncheon. Displaying this set on a blue table cloth with blue candles in crystal candle holders is truly eye appealing. **Left to right:** candle holders, pair, $16; bowls, crimped, 5-1/2", $9; luncheon plates, 8-3/8", $15; cups, $8 each; saucers, $6 each.

THE SEARCH FOR
THE ELUSIVE JUBILEE

Of all the patterns of Depression Glass, "Jubilee," manufactured by the Lancaster Glass Company in 1930 has collectors searching most frantically for this elegant glassware. Elaborately decorated with an exquisite floral engraving, it can be displayed with great pride and admired by all glass lovers.

After inheriting the basic luncheon set from a dear neighbor, I have become an avid collector of "Jubilee." Not knowing what this lovely topaz glassware was, I immediately began to research and search for it. I soon learned that this Lancaster pattern was inspired by Frigidaire's 15th Anniversary, and its name commemorated that "Jubilee." With the complete luncheon set a card was enclosed stating, "Please accept this Jubilee Luncheon Service with the compliments of your Frigidaire Dealer." That is how this elegant glassware was distributed.

This pattern was produced in a soft topaz and pink color with an elegant flower and leaf design containing twelve petals with an open center. The petals are usually sharp but can sometimes be rounded. All of the petals have the same length with no small petals between each larger petal. This describes the TRUE Jubilee. Never has a pattern caused so much controversy as to what

Display of the basic luncheon set. A very exquisite pattern in a soft topaz or pink featuring an elegant flower and leaf design with twelve petals with an open center. A beautiful set to display or use with pride. Tumblers, 6", 10 oz., $43 each. Luncheon plates, 8-3/4", $16. Creamer, $23, sugar, $23. Cups, $16 each. Saucers, $7 each.

constitutes Jubilee. If you collectors should be successful in finding pink Jubilee, remember these pieces have the Jubilee open center flower etched with sixteen petals of even length.

There are a number of "look-alike" pieces that confuse collectors who do not observe this pattern closely. Actually, these "look-alike's" are very attractive and can be used in harmony with the Jubilee items. They are more plentiful and less expensive. With the scarcity and exorbitant prices of Jubilee many collectors are willing to accept these similar items.

What amazes me is how the search for this pattern goes on and on in spite of finding less or nothing at shows and flea markets. This proves the collector's persistence.

I have had a problem finding the serving pieces due to scarcity, intense collector demand, and the escalating prices. Searching for Jubilee from east to west it took a year to find the elusive pink thirteen-inch sandwich plate at the Don Wirk show in Portland, Oregon. What a glorious find and a treasure forever.

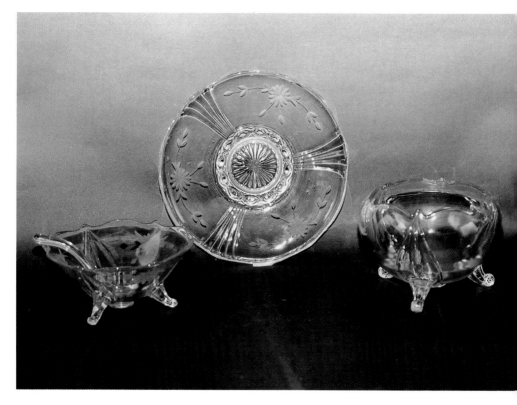

"Look-a-Like" pieces. In the 1930s the Lancaster Company produced a lot of this elegant glassware in topaz with similar designs. **Left to right:** mayonnaise bowl with ladle, 6-1/2", $20; plate, 8-1/2", $12; rose bowl, 3-footed, tear effect design, 5-1/4", $15.

In my quest for Jubilee, I decided to ask various dealers at flea markets if they had any pieces of this glassware. One Sunday, attending a flea market at a city only a few miles from my home town, I approached a dealer about my interest in Jubilee and if she was familiar with it. Much to my surprise she told me immediately that she had the 11" center-handled sandwich tray with the tear design at her shop. Within a few days it was in my possession. Needless to say I was elated over the purchase because it is elegant and rare. Just a short time later while browsing through a local antique shop I spied an object which I thought looked like the Jubilee Candlestick. As I reached further back in the case there was the pair in "mint" condition. It is interesting that when one item of a pattern is found another surfaces soon after. This has been characteristic in my search of Depression Glass.

The treasured and hard to find 13" Jubilee pink sandwich plate with the creamer and the sugar. These pieces are difficult to find. Sandwich plate, pink, 13-1/2", $75-85. Creamer, pink, $30-40. Sugar, $30-40.

The 11" center handled tray. This is a very elegantly designed piece of glassware with the tear effect. Another hard to find item in Jubilee. Tray, center handled, 11", $200-225.

Candle holders. This is a very attractive pair which compliments the whole set of Jubilee. A beauty to display. Topaz, $160-175. This is another hard to find item in this pattern.

BERRY BOWLS

Berry bowl sets have always intrigued me. In my search for them, I usually find the large bowl first and then hunt for the small individual ones. Many collectors find the small bowls and then search for the large berry bowl.

A berry set is defined as a large bowl, with a standard size of 8", and matching smaller bowls which are usually 4-1/2".

My interest stems from the "Adam" set which I inherited from my mother. This beautiful rose pink, delicate garden-type pattern bowl adorned the center of our table for supper, a lighter meal. The bowl was filled with various kinds of canned fruit or sauces. Peach sauce was the popular favorite of my family. Surrounding the dinner or luncheon plates were the individual bowls for serving. This "Adam" berry bowl set is extremely attractive with the center group of alternating feathers and plumes and the wide radial ridges and wide rims. The square shape of the bowls with slightly indented corners is unique. Square shapes were popular in this period, 1932-1934. Adam was produced by the Jeannette Glass Company in the 1930s. Every Easter I use this set for a special salad.

In "Bubble" collectors can choose iridescent, crystal, blue, white and amber. The berry bowls in this pattern are a delight to collect, easy to identify, and

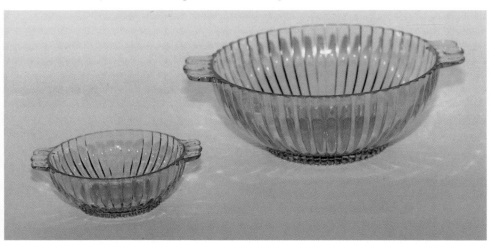

The various sets are versatile and fun to use for serving salads, desserts, and fruits. They are perfect. All of these I use daily and especially for the holidays. These sets will always remain popular with me. A berry bowl set is made up of a large bowl and several smaller bowls. This set was made in the middle 1930s. It has vertical ribs, sunburst bottom and closed handles and is similar to "Queen Mary". Small bowl, 4-1/2", $8. Large bowl, 8", $25.

quite available. The iridescent is not as available, but is beginning to surface. The very common white is wonderful to use with fruits and Jello. I use these sets over and over again and have had good luck collecting.

"Burple" in crystal and green is another popular and beautifully designed bowl which is slightly footed. The green set, when used at Christmas, gives the table a festive look. "Royal Ruby," is a very rich looking set perfect for Christmas and Valentines Day. My family enjoys this set which I call my "Holiday Dessert Set." This was one of Hocking's first berry sets, along with Sandwich design in 1939 and 1940.

Coronation, "Banded Fine Rib," deep red and very attractive, is also used for the holidays. Its open handles and the sunburst of radial lines surrounded by larger, more widely spaced lines, are attractive features of these bowls. The border is an inner circle of ridges with a plain outer band. This berry set is more easily found since it was manufactured for a special sales promotion.

The crystal berry bowl sets are brilliant, quite available and durable. They blend in very well with the various colored patterns.

Besides being attractive, berry bowls are very versatile. They can be used for salads, soups, cereals, ice cream, puddings, fresh fruits and various snacks. The large berry bowl and the small matching bowls work equally well for serving popcorn. With a little ingenuity, these sets can be put to much use, even individually for many purposes. The large berry, sometimes called the "master" bowl, is an ideal serving bowl. The smaller bowls can be used for numerous servings.

Adam, Jeannette Glass Co., 1932-1934. Bowl, pink, 9", $25. Bowls, 4-3/4", $14.

"Bubble," Anchor Hocking 1940-1965. Large berry bowl, 8-3/8", $12. Fruit bowls, 4-1/2", $4. The 4-1/2" fruit constitutes this set in iridescent. This is a scarce item.

Many collectors find themselves with these small bowls and don't realize that they are part of a set. For beginning collectors sizes of the large berry and the small berry can be confusing. The smaller bowls are listed as dessert 4-3/4" and
4-3/8", and a sauce 5", and a berry only 3-3/4". There's also a 4" berry, a 4-5/8", 4-1/4", 5", 5-1/4" and 5-1/2". The 5-1/2" can be mistaken for the cereal bowl which is usually 5" to 5-1/2". Cereal bowls are deeper but can be used with a large berry bowl. Interestingly, in one pattern, Colonial, "Knife and Fork", there are two sizes of berry bowls 3-3/4" and 4-1/2". In some patterns you can find the small berry bowls without the large berry bowl and the large berry bowl without the small berry bowls.

The large berry bowl is often listed as a salad or a fruit bowl. The sizes vary from 7-1/2" to 10". A salad or fruit bowl is usually 8-3/4" and deep. In one pattern, "Daisy" by Indiana, there are two sizes of the large berry, 7-3/8" and 9-3/8". Even though the sizes vary, the sets can still be put together and are a delight to collect.

I have started other patterns and enjoy immensely the hunt, even if I find only one. Recently I found the "Heritage" berry bowl, a little more difficult to find, and am now searching for the small bowls.

For all collectors, there is a problem that you may encounter in collecting these sets. From the daily usage and the stacking, the inner rims were vulnerable to chipping and must be checked thoroughly. In spite of this, the bowls in the various shapes, hexagonal, octagonal, scalloped, flat, curved, beaded, ruffled, crimped, round, square and footed are fascinating to collect.

"Bubble," Anchor Hocking, 1940-1965. Large berry bowl, crystal, 8-3/8", $7. Fruit bowls, 4-1/2", $4. Crystal is more available. The 4" bowl, is more difficult to find. A very versatile set.

"Bubble," Anchor Hocking, 1940-1965. Large berry bowl, blue, 8-3/8", $16. Fruit bowls, blue, 4-1/2", $12. This is the popular color and is snatched up very quickly.

"Bubble," Anchor Hocking, 1940-1965. Produced later in the 1950s. Attractive in serving fruits. Large berry bowl, white, 8-3/8", $6. Fruit bowls, white, 4-1/2", $4.

"Burple," Anchor Hocking Glass Co., 1940-1950. Very attractive dessert set for a festive Christmas setting. Large bowl, 8-1/2", $15. Small bowls, 4-5/8", $4.

Royal Ruby, Anchor Hocking Glass Co., 1938-1960s; 1977. A beautiful "Holiday" set for serving and displaying. Large bowl, 8-1/2", $18. Small bowls, 4-1/4" to 4-1/2", $5.

Coronation, "Banded Rib," Saxon Hocking Glass Co., 1936-1940. A very attractive set with the open handles, and a rich, dark red color. Large berry bowl, handled, 8", $16. Small bowls with handles, 4-1/4", $6.

An exquisitely designed berry bowl set made in the middle 1930s. Purchased from an estate sale. Large bowl, 8-1/2", $20. Small bowl, 4-3/4", $6.

One thing that never ceases to amaze me are the advertisements for seven piece berry sets in various patterns and colors selling for less than a dollar. Many of these berry sets were manufactured for "special sales" promotions.

THE GLAMOUR OF CANDLESTICKS

Candlesticks come in the various shapes, from the single flat to the square one light and two light. The variety of colors from black to pink added a touch of color in the bleak Depression era. **Back row left to right:** Amethyst, $10; Oyster & Pearl, $50; Royal Ruby, Iris, "Iris & Herringbone," iridescent, $42 pr.; Oyster & Pearl, pink, $22. **Middle row left to right:** amber candlesticks, $8; black, Fenton "Saw Tooth," $20; red & amber, $20. **Front row left to right:** Mt. Pleasant, "Double Shield," $25; swirled candlesticks, Amber, $5 single; Pink, $12 pr.

Another of my favorite forms of Depression Glass are the endless variety of glamorous candlesticks. The era of the 1920s and 1930s was a great one for candlesticks. In colors or in brilliant crystal, candlesticks brought a little romance and glamour to the drab and worried times. Many sets were bought as gift items or were received as premiums.

Candlesticks were produced in specific patterns from "Adam" to "Windsor Diamond" and matched the dinner sets. The table setting was not complete without them. I must admit that I feel the same way. I recently served an anniversary dinner in "Blue Bubble" complete with blue tapers in the crystal "Bubble" candlesticks. My guests were extremely impressed with this beautiful setting.

Candlesticks came in a variety of shapes including flat, straight edge, rolled edge, ruffled edge, round footed, octagon footed, dolphin footed, mushroom, saucer, square and column.

Among the most unique and highly prized candlesticks ever produced are those of the elegant glassware lines produced during the Depression era and into the 1950s. This glassware, etched, handmade and exquisitely designed, was sold in the jewelry stores and department stores. These elegant candlesticks are admired and eagerly sought after by many glass collectors. The companies producing this elegant glassware were Cambridge, Duncan and Miller, Fostoria, Heisey, Imperial, Morgan Town, Paden City, and Tiffin Glass.

In the "American" pattern there are at least 11 different types from twin to the Eiffel Tower candlesticks. "Candlewick" has a variety of candleholders with the unique finger hold, 3-light on circle beaded center, a handled with bowled up vase, flower and flower epergne. It also has the mushroom, rolled edge, the urn, and 6" holders on circular centered bead. "Crystolite" has the unusual candle-block, 1-light square, swirl, and the vase 3-light type.

I am totally charmed with the candlestick that has several branches for candles with the 2-light or 3-light. "Baroque" is typical of this truly magnificent candlestick.

Extremely charming is the elaborate candelabrum 1, 2, and 3 light bell base with bobeche and prisms. A bobeche *(bobesh French)* is a dish or a shallow cup with a hole in it, that fits around a candle at the base to catch melted wax. Prisms are transparent crystals, usually with 3-sided ends, that separate white light passing through it into the colors of the rainbow. The most magnificent are the candelabras in the "Sandwich" pattern from the 1-light with bobeche and prisms to the 5-light.

The "Rose" pattern has the most elaborate candlestick of the Heisy glassware, the classic 6" deep epergnette on a 3-light candlestick. This is truly exquisite and very rare. What a prize to find or to own. An épergne or épergnette is an ornamental dish with specific tiers, branches, or divisions to hold fruit, candy, or flowers. This highly coveted piece is used primarily as a centerpiece for a dining table or a buffet.

I have candlesticks on display in almost every room of my house. Changing the colors of the candles is a big thing with me. Candlesticks provide the perfect accent for the holidays. They play a great role in my decorative scheme, red, green, blue, amber, and white. With or without candles, they give a distinc-

Some of the white candles in different shapes. The companies producing these candles were Westmoreland Glass Company, 1943-present, and Anchor Hocking Glass Company 1941-1946. **Left to right:** milk glass, ruffled tops, cupped, $10 pr.; milk glass, stemmed with grape pattern, $12 pr.; Moonstone, $16 pr.; Silver Crest, white with crystal edge low, ruffled, $22.

tive look on tables, organ, piano, fireplace, desk, dresser, and chests. They add a special sparkling accent on tables and buffets. Using your own creativity, candles can offer decorative appeal. The glamour and romance of the candlesticks still prevails in this era, too.

A variety of crystal one- and two-light candlesticks. The patterns were produced by the Federal Glass Company in 1928, Jeannette Glass Company 1928-1932, 1950s-1970s, Hocking Glass Company, 1936-1949 and Anchor Hocking Glass Company 1939-1941. These brilliant crystal candlesticks enlightened the depressing era. **Back row left to right:** Iris, Iris & Herringbone, $42; two-light with center cup, $15; "Queen Mary," double branch, $15. **Front row left to right:** two-light pair, elegant, $15; Windsor, "Windsor Diamond," pair, $20; circular beaded, $10; "Manhattan," square, 4-1/2", $15.

Another group of crystal candlesticks, mainly pairs in different designs in one, two and three light. Many of these sets were gift items or premiums and were produced by the Federal Glass Company. At the right front is Oyster and pearl, $22. Others range in value from $10-20.

This is the beautiful blue Bubble set that I use for special dinners. The crystal candlesticks with the long, blue tapering candles add the touch of elegance to this table setting. **Left to right:** candlesticks, crystal, $16 pr.; cup and saucer, $7; dinner plate, 9-3/8", $8; bread and butter plate, 6-3/4", $4; creamer, $35; sugar, $20. **Front center:** fruit bowl, 4-1/2", $12.

Elegant candlesticks. Many of these were produced by the Imperial Glass Company, 1936-1984, and the Fostoria Glass Company, 1915-1986. These are all unique in style. Center candle with cup inserts, unique. $10-20.

Candlewick, line #400, produced by Imperial Glass Company, 1936-1984. This is a very unique pair with fingerhold and large beaded style. "Candlewick" has a variety of candle holder styles, some very elegant. $37 pr.

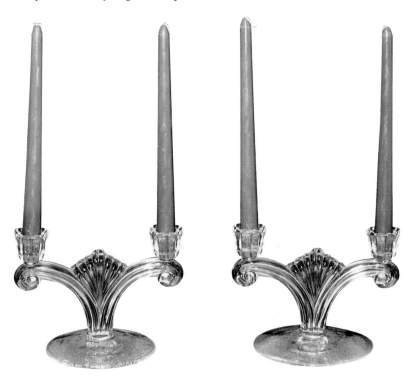

This two-light double branch pair, Cherokee Rose, with the delicate rose etched design on the bottom is my favorite to display. This set was produced by the Tiffin Glass Company 1940s-1950s, $70-80.

Another favorite is this very elegant three-light in a swirled, lined and ornate designed candle holder. This set was produced in crystal in the 1930s and is a beauty to display with various colored candles. $60-85 pr.

SHERBETS ARE FUN

Cobalt blue sherbet in the "Moderntone" pattern, by Hazel Atlas Glass Co., 1934-1942, and 1940s-1950s. This pressed pattern typifies the decorative art style of the 1930s. It has widely spaced concentric rings and was modern for its time. Cobalt blue, $14.

Collecting the endless variety of sherbets that were produced during the Depression Era is fun. On any shelf, in a hutch or curio, they make a colorful and interesting collection. In addition to their decorative value, my sets are put to good use serving fruits, ice cream, sherbet, puddings, cereals, salads, and even snacks.

A sherbet is a small ice cream or dessert dish, usually footed, or a dish with a long stem used to hold frozen desserts.

Sherbets come in various shapes including round-V, high and low thin-stemmed, low footed, bend footed, scalloped edge, ruffled edge, straight rim, flared rim, cupped rim, square type and the cone. Sherbets with the beaded bottom, scalloped base and the pattern etched on the bottom are very attractive. Some have the design on the inside and on the outside. Some shapes are unique and represent the eating habits of the United States during a particular time in our history. For example, when the radio began to advertise jello products, companies began to produce the numerous sherbets (I still serve Jello in sherbets). Many of the sets of dishes were not complete without the sherbets. They were used daily like the berry bowls and cereal bowls.

Some sherbets were designed to fit in a sherbet plate. Some fit in an off-center ring, like the pattern Ring, "Banded Ring," and Mayfair, which is a thin-blown sherbet that fits into an indented plate. These plates are usually 6-1/2" and can be easily confused with saucers. Collectors of sherbets need to be very careful to observe this. Also confusing is the fact that some sugar bowls do not have handles and therefore resemble a sherbet. The Rose Mary, "Dutch Rose" pattern in the sherbet is an example. It is actually an oddity and resembles a footed tumbler, too. I'm sure there are others out there.

Tall sherbets are known as Sherbet/Champagne and the Sherbet/Saucer Champagne. These are very elegantly styled and belong to the elegant glassware line.

The sizes of sherbets vary from 2-3/4" to 6-1/2". Most common and prevalent are the sizes from 2-3/4" to 4-1/2". I prefer this size for my servings. In many of the patterns there are two styles of sherbets, 4" low footed and 4-1/2" low footed. Some have the 4-5/8" tall, 3-3/8" diameter and 4-7/8" tall, 3-5/8" diameter. Dogwood "Apple Blossom" has three styles, low footed, low flared footed and tall footed. One pattern lists the sherbet, 3-1/2 oz. footed, as an egg cup. There are sherbets found in metal holders, but collectors prefer all glass sherbets.

Colors range from pink, yellow, topaz, amber, green, red, light blue, cobalt, jade, crystal, amethyst, black and white. I love the fired-on colors in the Moderntone pattern. I use them in the assorted colors for my breakfast table where they are ideal for serving fruits. The pattern Lincoln Inn has a big variety of colors, including black. What a nice collection that would be.

I have had so much fun collecting and searching for sherbets, whether to go with a set or to use individually. They can still be found, although some are becoming more scarce. The "Parrot," Sylvan sherbet, measuring 4-1/2" high, is so rare that it sells for $1,000. What a "find" that would be! I love the challenge of collecting sherbets.

Most Depression Glass sherbets fall into range of the modest budget, which is good news for collectors. They are small enough that, even with limited space, there will always be a place for them. One can collect just one of every variety which would still be fun and challenging.

These are the various shapes of the sherbets from flat to stem. All of these have a different design and are ideal for serving fruits, puddings and desserts. **Left to right:** Sandwich, footed, $9; Moonstone, footed, $7; Manhattan, low, $6; Silver Crest, stemmed, $11; Waterford Waffle, $4; Queen Mary, $5; Crackle Glass, $4.

Sherbets are bright and attractive in the various colors. Colors range from pink to dark green. These colored sherbets certainly enlightened this drab period. Very versatile and attractive on the tables. **Back row left to right:** Royal Ruby, $8; Daisy, footed, $5; Circle, $5; Floral and Diamond, $7; Loraine, basket, $31; Spiral, $5; solid green, $3. **Front row left to right:** Coronation, "Banded Rib," $5; Madrid, $8; Royal Ruby, $7; Florentine, No. 2. Poppy, $11; Forest Green, $7.

Elegant tall sherbets called sherbet/champagne. All of these are very attractive and elegantly styled and produced by the Heisey and Cambridge Glass Companies. $12 each.

These sherbets are the popular sizes, a size that I prefer for servings. The colors are also nice especially the red and green for the holidays. "Daisy" with the square bottom is unique. **Left to right:** Royal Ruby, 3", $7; Daisy, amber, 3", $5; Spiral, 5", $5; Forest Green, 2-3/4", $7; Coronation, "Banded Rib", "Saxon", 2-1/4", $5.

Hard to Find Sherbets. Some of the sherbets are becoming elusive. The "Jubilee" sherbet is a very delicate piece and scarce. "Starlight" sherbets have always been hard to find. Iris, "Iris and Herringbone," the very hot pattern in Depression Glass, has hard-to-find pieces and the prices are soaring due to the popularity. This sherbet is very attractive. **Left to right:** Jubilee, $65-70; Starlight, $14; Iris, Iris & Herringbone, iridescent, $15.

These sherbets in the Hobnail pattern in pink are scarce due to the small number produced. Very attractive for serving with crystal or white. Known for its longevity. Hobnail, Hocking Glass Company, 1934-1936. $3.

The fired-n sherbets in Modernstone's various colors are fun to collect and can be used with any crystal setting or individually. The colors are fascinating. Moderntone, Hazel Atlas Glass Co., 1934-1942. Late 1940s, early 1950s. 3-1/4", $4.

CREAMERS AND SUGARS
The Mainstay of Depression Glass

Among the popular favorites of glass produced during the Depression Era was an abundance of creamers and sugars. These bright, colorful and uniquely designed sets are highly collectible today.

Along with salt and pepper shakers and the butter dish, creamers and sugars were the focal point of the table settings. Today we still revere the creamers and sugars with our sets of dishes.

Available in all the Depression Glass colors, pink, amethyst, ruby, green, topaz, black, iridescent, primrose yellow, amber and cobalt blue, the shapes of creamers and sugars have a wide variety. They were made in round, oblong, oval, rectangular, cone, hexagonal, diamond, plain bottom and square footed.

Scalloped edges, pie crust edges, pointed edges, and paneled edges, provided attractive variations, as did designs of bubbles, spirals, swirls, diamond blocks, cubes, horizontal and vertical ribs, waffle, scrolls, circles and hobnobs. These designs give the creamers and sugars a special charm all their own.

The variety of sizes of creamers and sugars in the various patterns is interesting and a little frustrating. Sizes vary from 2-1/2" to 5". In the pattern "Moondrops," the creamer is available in a 2-3/4" miniature size and a 3-3/4" regular size. The sugar came in 2-3/4" and 4" sizes. In American Pioneer creamers are 2-3/4" and 3-1/2" and the sugars, 2-3/4" and 3-1/2". Cube, "Cubist" cream-

This setting of the sugar, creamer, salt and pepper shakers and the butter dish, still remains the focal point of our table setting. Even though we eat at a faster pace and the family meal is not as significant, these pieces still serve a purpose. Waterford "Waffle." **Left to right:** sugar, $10; salt shaker, $5; butter dish, $25; pepper shaker, $5; creamer, $4.

The variety of colors in the different shapes of the creamers and sugars certainly added color to the drab homes with the tables so colorful. **Back row left to right:** Royal Ruby, flat, $18; Daisy, footed, $17 pr.; Ring, "Banded Ring," $9 pr. **Front row left to right:** Floragold, "Louisa," $15 pr.; Newport, hairpin creamer, $12; Moderntone, creamer, $12; Swirl, "Petal Swirl," ultra-marine, $31 pr.

ers are 2-5/8" and 3-9/16" and sugars, 2-3/8" and 3". Georgian, "Love Birds" creamers are 3" and 4" and sugars 3" and 4". Colonial "Knife and Fork" has a big 5" creamer that is commonly called a milk pitcher, holding 18 oz. In the "Aurora" pattern there is no sugar, just a creamer 4-1/2" which is labeled a milk pitcher.

The styles of the handles are also interesting. The common styles are closed, open, lightening bolted, bead, scroll ball, and pointed. The Pretzel handle is very unusual with the round small open hole. When I serve my guests with the set they are fascinated with the handle.

Very odd are the sugar bowls without handles. Typical of this is Rosemary, "Dutch Rose," sometimes mistaken for a sherbet or a tumbler. Mayfair has a Federal footed sugar with no handles and to me it resembles a large sherbet. They are unique to that type. With my love for collecting sherbets, this has been confusing to me. Again, one must have a firm knowledge of the precise pieces of the various patterns. Many have believed these sugar bowls without handles to be spooners. It could be used as such but spooners appear to be larger.

Sugar lids are a challenging enigma for collectors. Lids in mint condition can be extremely expensive and worth more than the bottoms. This certainly holds true when the price of the Mayfair sugar lid is worth $1500 in pink and $1100 in green and yellow. When I discovered these prices I was shocked. Imagine finding this in Mayfair "Open Rose." Another thing to remember about the sugar lids is that they are interchangeable with the candy dishes.

Among the oddities of Depression Glass are creamers without spouts, which are called mugs. Some companies did have creamers without spouts and there is at least one two-spouted creamer known. Spouts were applied by hand using a wooden tool at many factories. This could explain why some have a more pronounced lip than others.

The trays that hold the creamer and sugar are classic and distinctive. I cherish the center handled tray in the Tea Room, the domino tray in "Round Robin" (so unusual, with the creamer in the center ring surrounded by sugar cubes), and the Cameo "Ballerina," or "Dancing Girl" domino sugar tray.

Creamers and sugars are fun and very challenging to collect. If the collector is limited for space or funds, these will certainly fit in. Right now, I'm on the hunt for the lids and the scarce creamers and sugars to match my sets. I think I have a real challenge ahead of me; but then, isn't that what collecting is all about?

More colors and shapes. The light with a trace of color are attractive. The black color was very popular and very striking with white, but difficult to find today. **Back row left to right:** "Ouide," $8 pr.; Newport, "Hairpin," $6 pr. **Front row left to right:** Cameo, "Ballerina," $18; Block Optic, "Block," $12; Mt. Pleasant, "Double Shield," $15; "Moonstone," $16 pr.

White sugars and creamers in some very unusual shapes. **Back row left to right:** "Forget-Me-Not," $8 pr.; Hazel Atlas, Indiana Custard, $7 pr.; "Flower & Leaf," Newport, "Hairpin," $6 pr. **Center:** "Daisy" white, sugar, $3. **Front center:** the oval pair, Vitrock with "Flower Rim," is very unusual in shape. $8 pr.;

Green, the typical Depression color, appeared in a variety of forms. **Back row left to right:** Elegant, $10 pr.; Depression, $8 pr. **Middle row left to right:** Sunflower, $38 pr.; Forest Green, $12 pr.; Sharon, "Cabbage Rose," sugar, $16. **Front row left to right:** Georgian, "Lovebirds," $26 pr.; Floral & Diamond Band, sugar, $14.

Pink, a very popular color then and today, has a big variety even in the elegant line. All of the shapes are so unique and are soaring in price. **Back row left to right:** Cube, "Cubist," $5 pr. Sharon, "Cabbage Rose," $35; Doric, $24. **Front row left to right:** Manhattan, $24 pr.; Sunflower, $38 pr.; Queen Mary, $16 pr.

Back row left to right: Manhattan, "Horizontal Ribbed," $21 pr.;
Moderntone, "Wedding Band," concentric rings, $8. **Middle row left to right:** Ring, "Banded Ring," horizontal ribbed bands, circle pattern, $9 pr.; Queen Mary, vertical ribbed, crystal, $10 pr. **Front row left to right:** Starlight, waffle design with cross-over stippled lines giving a plaid effect, $10.

A variety of unusual shapes in creamers and sugars, including diamond-shaped facets, bubbles, hobnails, flowers surrounded by a pineapple and a pressed type pattern. **Left:** Windsor, "Windsor Diamond" diamond, shaped facets of 4 larger bands, $12. **Back center:** "Bubble," scalloped edges, radial sunburst in a circle of bull's eye dots, $11 pr. **Back right:** "Miss America," Hobnail motif, large sunburst of radial lines, $17 pr. **Front center:** "Pineapple & Floral" center motif is a flower surrounded by a pineapple floral border. $14 pr. **Front right:** "Sandwich," $16. All over stippling spaced around flower, foliage scroll motifs in elaborate design.

Creamers and sugars in the elegant glassware line, with their beaded handles, floral designs, or vertical ribs. **Back row left to right:** Candlewick, flat, beaded handle, $27 pr.; Crystal etched, floral, $12. **Front row left to right:** Crystal etched, floral, $12; Crystolite, $35 pr.

Hard to find creamers and sugars. The crystal Iris, "Iris and Herringbone" in the back row is more available than the blue "Bubble." The creamer in blue "Bubble" is extremely scarce. "Jubilee" in topaz and pink in the front row is not only scarce but escalating in price. **Back row left to right:** Iris, "Iris and Herringbone," crystal, $25 pr.; "Bubble," blue, $53 pr. **Front row left to right:** Jubilee, topaz, $45 pr.; Jubilee, pink, $70 pr.

Tray sets for sugars and creamers. **Left:** "Sandwich" set, $16. **Back center:** "National," $20. **Back right:** "Fenton," $20. **Front right:** "Cubist," $10. **Front leftt:** "American," $25-30.

"Aurora," Hazel Atlas Glass Company, late 1930s, in cobalt blue is interesting due to its size, which is larger than the average creamer. For that reason it is labeled as a milk pitcher. Many collectors prefer to call it that. There is no sugar to match the creamer. $22.

"Pretzel," No. 622, Indiana Glass Co., late 1930s-1980s. This pattern fascinates my guests. The style of the handle with the round small hole intrigues them. Creamer, $4; sugar, $4.

It is interesting to learn that some sugars were produced without handles, as in this set. It has a hobnail bottom. Sugar, $5; creamer, $5.

THE BEAUTY OF THE CONSOLE SET

My love and fascination for candlesticks of the Depression Era carries over into the elegant console sets. A console is a centerpiece bowl usually with candlesticks or vases. The sets with vases are more generally elegant in style. The size of the large bowl varies from 9 to 14 inches. It is also called a garniture set.

These sets were extremely popular as centerpieces for the dining table or buffet. I can recall seeing many of these elegant sets on buffets, and they certainly added a touch of glamour and romance to the setting.

They were manufactured in the typical colors of the Depression Era: blue, pink, green, amber, crystal, amethyst, yellow, topaz, iridescent, red, black and opalescent. The intricate etched designs are very impressive, appearing lace-like on the crystal or colored glass.

Consoles were produced in a variety of shapes including the stem base, three- or four-footed, flared, round, crimp, rolled edge, octagon, flat top, deep, oval, flanged rim, cupped, and two handled. In the "Bowman" set, 10-1/2", the bowl is reversible, uniquely suited for dual purposes. The candlesticks are 1-1/2".

Some consoles have a matching salad plate, making a very attractive combination. The bowl can remain on the buffet holding fruit, while the plate can be used for something else. These sets were introduced in 1925. One interesting version has a smaller console bowl with a wide rim. One could serve more off the rim than the bowl, making it a novel and rare item.

This bowl with the candlestick constitutes a console set. These make beautiful center pieces and were very popular in the 1920s and 1930s. Garniture sets, as they were called, came in a variety of colors and unique shapes. Deep Oyster and Pearl crystal fruit bowl, 10-1/2," $22. Candle holders, crystal, $18.

"Candlewick" has three console sets. It is rare to find all three pieces intact and together, but if you find the bowl you can enjoy the hunt for matching candlesticks or vice versa. Actually, I have had luck finding the candlesticks first.

There is such beauty in the console sets that I have them on display most of the time. I use them with or without the candlesticks. For the various seasons and holidays they are ideal for decorating.

Many of the console bowls have a satinized finish with floral patterns. Satin finish, or frost, is a 19th century term for glass with a matte finish. It was also advertised as "plush glass" or "velvet glass." These pieces were dipped in camphoric acid, which created a soft dull finish, "satinizing" them. Some bowls had hand-painted flowers which are usually worn off. These, of course, can't be classified as in "mint" condition. While most of these bowls still have an appealing look, some collectors are turned off by the worn look and avoid them entirely. The prices are definitely less for the satin or frosted finish pieces, sometimes by as much as 30 or 40 percent.

As I think back, seeing these gracefully shaped, exquisitely styled and etched console sets in the various pleasing colors, I feel that these are the most coveted of the Depression Glass shapes and variety. There is beauty in each of them, and they are slowly gaining more devotees.

It is something of a shock to come across advertising that offers three piece console sets in rose and green, with a 10-1/2" rolled bowl with the wide base and the 3-1/2" candlesticks, for less than a dollar. Yes, this for a complete set. Another advertisement mentions a Dollar Day special for the complete console set. As we collectors would say, "What a steal."

This set, Iris, "Iris and Herringbone" by the Jeannette Glass Company 1928-1932, 1950s and 1970s, is highly collectible in crystal and iridescent. The unusual large spray of Iris with the blade like leaves emanating from one point at the inner rim creates a bouquet effect. Crystal fruit bowl, ruffled, 11", $15.
Candlesticks, crystal, $42 pr.

This is the attractive console set in iridescent Iris, "Iris and Herringbone." Many collectors prefer the iridescent color over the crystal. Fruit bowl, ruffled, 11", $15. Candlesticks, iridescent, $42 pr.

The milk glass console sets are very attractive, especially with the grape pattern. Some have the high column candlesticks. The white bowls can be nicely decorated. West-moreland and Imperial Glass Companies produced many of these sets. Bowl with clusters of grapes and leaves, heavy, 10", $20. Candlesticks with grapes and leaves, 4-3/4", $10.

This is the fired-on color in Oyster and Pearl. They also came in pink and green with white. Many collectors dislike the fired-on colors but I think they are attractive with the white. Console set, Oyster and Pearl, bowl, 10-1/2", $12, candle holders, $12.

This is the popular Silver Crest set, a very white glassware with the crystal edge. The ruffle and double crimp edging makes this pattern attractive. Fenton Art Company produced a big line of this and it is still in production. 1943 to present. Bowl, 11", $46; Candle holders, low, ruffled, $20 pr.

This is a beautiful round flared rimmed bowl in the popular Nu Green color, produced by the Bartlett-Collins Co., Sapulpa, Oklahoma, 1927-1931. It has also been called a flower bowl, and is very versatile for decorating and also for serving fruits. There are also candle holders for this bowl. Console bowl, round, flared rim, 12", $20.

The salad bowl and plate is a very popular centerpiece. I often display these for the seasons and holidays, and for luncheons. Both can be used for numerous purposes and are fun to collect and display. Oyster and Pearl, deep crystal fruit bowl, 10-1/2", $22; crystal sandwich plate, 13-1/2", $18.

This Royal Ruby console is my favorite to display for the holidays. The rich deep red on a white table cloth makes a very festive setting. The bowl and plate are becoming difficult to find. Bowl, scarce, 11-1/2", $32; plate, scarce, 13-3/4", $35.
candlesticks, three-footed, red to amber, 4", $20 pr.

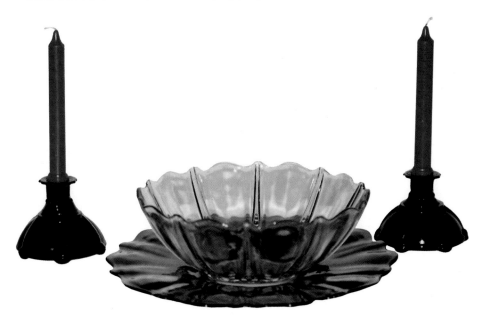

This is Oyster and Pearl console set with crystal bowl, royal ruby plate, and royal ruby candlesticks. The royal ruby in this pattern is difficult to find. Deep fruit bowl, crystal, 10-1/2", $22; sandwich plate, royal ruby. 13-1/2", $45; candlesticks, royal ruby, $50.

The Oyster and Pearl console set in pink is an elegant set to display. This is one of my favorites in this pattern. It never fails to attract my guests' attention. Produced by Anchor Hocking Glass Co., 1938-1940. Bowl, 10-1/2", $22; plate, 13-1/2", $18; candle holders, pink, 3-1/2", $22 pr.

This is unusual but very elegant in a console set. The cornucopia vases are especially so. Produced by Heisey. Vases, 9", $50-60 pr.; gondola fruit bowl with closed handles, 15-1/2", $20-25.

Reversible bowls with matching candlesticks were very popular in the 1920s and 1930s.
Many of these sets are so exquisitely designed with delicate etchings by Lancaster, Lotus,
U.S. Glass, Jeannette, L.E. Smith, Imperial and New Martinsville Companies.
This reversible bowl is in light purple with an etched design of birds at an ornate water
fountain. Very unusual bowl, $45.

A LOOK AT
DEPRESSION GLASS PLATES

The plate is the most ordinary, yet most indispensable piece of any set of Depression glass. As I started collecting sets of dishes, I was concerned primarily with the dinner, luncheon, and dessert plates. I was not really familiar with the other types of plates out there until I got deeper into this subject and began the hunt for the complete sets. I have found the collection and knowledge of these plates extremely interesting.

Plates come in various shapes: round, square, oval, hexagonal, rectangular, and octagonal. The rims of the plates can be flared, unflared, scalloped, fluted, petal shaped, cupped edge, rolled edge, serrated, and scroll edged.

Some sets of dishes have plates in a variety of sizes from a 6" dessert plate to a 13" chop plate. A complete set could have a 7" bread and butter plate, a 7-1/2" salad plate, an 8-9" luncheon plate, a 9" breakfast plate, and 10" dinner plate.

The dinner plate, the most familiar to everyone and the one from which we consume most of our food, is actually becoming scarce and expensive in many sets of Depression Glass. Very difficult to find right now are the plates in the "Old Cafe" pattern. This is a simple, but pleasing piece in one of the smaller patterns which features the dinner plate. "Forest Green," "Circle," "New Century," "S Pattern," "Stippled Rose Band," "Normandie," and "Bouquet and Lattice" are some of the other patterns where the dinner plates are difficult to find. Some of the smaller patterns do not have a dinner plate. To avoid disappointment in the collection of your sets, be sure to check out the patterns very thoroughly. Some of the sets without dinner plates are "Cube," "Cubist," "Aunt Polly," "Avocado," "Diamond Quilted," "Cloverleaf," "Coronation," "Columbia," "Hex Optic," "Floral and Diamond Band," "Fortune," "Hobnail," "Jubilee," "Moonstone," "Mt. Pleasant," "Newport," "Vernon," "Patrick," "Raindrops," "Radiance," "Ring," "Banded Ring," "Ribbon," "Roulette," "Round Robin," "Spiral," "Strawberry," and "Tea Room."

Interesting is the "Sunflower" pattern, which has only a dinner plate and a cake plate. "Patrician," made by the Federal Glass Company of the 1930s, has the largest dinner plate, 10-1/2". This plate was a premium item of the Depression Era which came with the purchase of a 10-pound bag of flour.

The standard size of the dinner plate is usually 10" to 10-1/2". However, there is a smaller dinner plate 9-1/2" in some sets. In Century, there are two sizes of dinner plates as is prevalent in most of Fostoria's pattern. The larger plate is the harder one to find. This larger plate was priced higher to start with so many people did without it. In "Lorraine Basket" there are two sizes of the dinner plate, 9-3/8" and 10-1/4". The green dinner plates are becoming increasingly hard to find. The green in "Lorraine Basket" seems to appeal to me. For any collector interested in collecting Homespun "Fine Rib," the dinner plates are not common.

The luncheon plate, used for light meals, is easier to collect because of its availability. The 7-9 inch plate is smaller than a dinner plate and larger than a salad plate. The standard measurement for this plate is 7-1/2" to 8". Luncheon plates are ideal for small lunches, a light breakfast, and for bridge club gatherings. Many patterns do not have the luncheon plates. They include: Anniversary, Cherry Blossom, Cremax, Chinex, Classic, Diana, Doric and Doric Pansy, Queen Mary, Princess, Rosemary Dutch Rose, Mayfair Manhattan and Sierra Pinwheel. In the patterns Floral and Diamond Band, and Fruits, the only plate available is the 8" luncheon plate. The exquisitely designed Jubilee luncheon plate, in the rich color topaz, is my favorite, and I serve on this with much pride to my guests. I am fortunate to have the double luncheon set.

Cake plates are very popular. This large serving plate or utility plate was significant to the various sets. The sizes of these plates vary from 10" to 13". Some patterns have two sizes, 11" and 13". The shapes also vary from pattern to pattern. They may be thin or heavy, and come in the flat style, with three legs, or as a pedestal plate, though this last type is rare. Some have a groove near the rim for the insertion of a lid, usually a metal or a glass cover. This is characteristic of the Snowflake cake, pink, 12-3/4". Some of the cake plates have very striking handles and some are plain. The cake plate in Mayfair "Open Rose" has unusual loop handles. Cameo "Ballerina" or "Dancing Girl" has two types of cakeplates, a 10" plate with legs and 10-1/2" flat plate. Sunflower, a very pretty pattern in pink and green, is quite plentiful, as it was a premium item packed in a 20-pound sack of flour for about four years. These I use constantly.

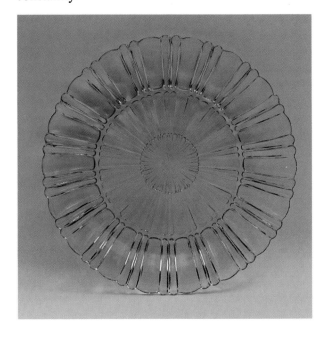

This is a 10" dinner plate in the pattern, Old Cafe, by the Hocking Glass Co. 1936-1940. It is a plain pattern, but not as plentiful as other patterns. It has a center sunburst surrounded by a circle of more widely spaced radiating lines. The rim has a series of wide plain panels with three narrow lined panels. This dinner plate is very scarce. Dinner plate, 10", $35.

127

Plates were made in a variety of shapes, from round to octagonal, and colors, from green to amber. These colors helped to brighten the homes. **Top row, left to right:** Forest Green, square dinner plate, 9-1/4", $27; scarce Royal Ruby, square plate, 8-3/8", $10; Moroccan Amethyst, octagonal dinner plate, $8. **Second row, left to right:** Jade-ite, round plate with pie crust edge, 9-1/8", $8; Daisy, round plate with daisies, 9-1/2", $6; Royal Ruby, round plate, 9-1/8", $12; Ouide, round, fired on yellow-black, 9", $9. **Third row, left to right:** Cremex, white with floral decoration, 9-3/4", $9; Daisy, amber, 9-1/2", $9; Horseshoe, elaborate design of scrollwork, 8-3/8", $12. **Bottom row, left to right:** Moderntone, swirled lines, 8-7/8", $12; Old Cafe, widely spaced lines, 10", $35.

Opposite page, bottom:
Types of plates include small salad, dinner, luncheon, salver and smaller serving plates. The salvers, 12" large non-handled serving plates were very popular. **Top, left to right:** American Sweetheart, salad plate, 8", $9; Petalware, monax, salad plate, decorated, $5; Chinex classic, dinner plate, plain, 9-3/4", $4; **Bottom, left to right:** Petalware, salver, decorated, 11", $11; "S" Pattern, "Stippled Rose Band," luncheon plate, 8-1/4", $6; Beaded edge plate, large dinner or smaller salver, 10-1/2", $30.

Some of the numerous patterns in the plates. **Top, left to right:** Manhattan, plate, horizontal ribbed, 10-1/4", $20; Waterford "Waffle", a lattice or waffle design, 9-5/8", $11; Queen Mary, vertical ribbed, 8-3/4", $5; Pretzel, No. 622, plate, scalloped rim with x's, 8-3/8", $5. **Bottom, left to right:** Miss America, hobnail motif, radial lines, 8-1/2", $7; Heritage, flower in center and petals in a beaded design in brilliant crystal, 8", $9; Bubble, scalloped edges, centers with a radial sunburst in a circle or bull's eye dots, 9-3/8", $8; Starlight, center has a waffle design, borders have cross over stippled lines giving a plaid effect, 9", $8.

Common plate sizes. Top left: Daisy, green, 7-3/8", $6. **Top right:** Bubble, bread & butter, blue, 6-3/4", $4. **Bottom left:** Bubble, dinner, blue, 9-3/8", $8. **Bottom right:** Diamond Quilted, luncheon, 8", $5-6.

These are large flat plates called chop plates, or, sometimes, salvers. The sizes are usually 13" to 13-3/4". These can be used for a variety of servings. **Left:** Windsor, "Windsor Diamond," Jeannette Glass Co. 1936-1946. Plate, 13-5/8", $46. **Right:** Floragold, "Louisa," Jeannette Glass Co. 1936-1946. Plate, 13-1/2", $23.

130

This sandwich plate with open handles, in Windsor, "Windsor Diamond" pressed pattern, imitates crystal, cut crystal. The series of facets emanate from a circle of radial ribs. Plate, sandwich, open handle, 10-1/4", $18.

The grill plate in Cameo, "Ballerina" or "Dancing Girl" is very striking in the yellow color. Also very unique with the human figure. This is one of the two styles, the other has tab handles. Grill plate in yellow, 10-1/2", $7.

This Princess grill plate, with the closed handles, in the octagonal shape with the center snowflake motif in the pattern, is very attractive, in pink. 9-1/2", $14.

Princess grill plate, with the closed handles in green. This is typical Depression green. 9-1/2", $14.

Hard To Find Plates; **Back left:** scarce Old Cafe dinner plate, 10", $35. **Back right:** "S" Pattern, "Stippled Rose Band," dinner plate, 9-1/4", $10. **Front:** Dinner plate, Forest Green, 9-1/4", $27.

Patrician, "Spoke," Federal Glass Co. 1933-1937. This dinner plate, in amber is available even though it is the largest in all of the patterns. A set can be completed. Federal Glass Co. 1933-1937. Dinner plate, amber, 10-1/2", $7.

Luncheon Plates. These plates, ranging in sizes from 8-1/4" to 8-3/4", are popular luncheon plates. They are the ideal size and attractive for luncheon serving. **Top left:** Heritage, 8", $9. Ideal for serving a luncheon. Very brilliant. **Top right:** Moonstone, 8-3/8", $15. Most attractive and produced for a luncheon set. **Bottom:** Jubilee, 8-3/4", $16. Exquisitely designed for a luncheon set.

This cake plate, in Princess, is one of the popular flat cake plates. This is a very sturdy cake plate in typical green color. Three legs, in green, 10", $20.

This is the elegant tray-like, 2 handled cake plate. The gentle curves of the plate and the uniquely shaped handles, along with the floral design, make this a beautiful serving piece. Jubilee tray, two-handled cake plate, topaz, 11", $47.

A beginner collector looking for a challenge and an unusual cake plate, can search for the Harp. These plates resemble the older pattern glassware. There are at least 10 different styles of this cake plate. The set is ideal for a dessert luncheon, if you can find the pieces.

Not only are cake plates attractive, they are also versatile. They can be used for serving various foods, from birthday cakes to small snacks. These are worth picking up in the pedestal style, as the flat cake plates have become so common.

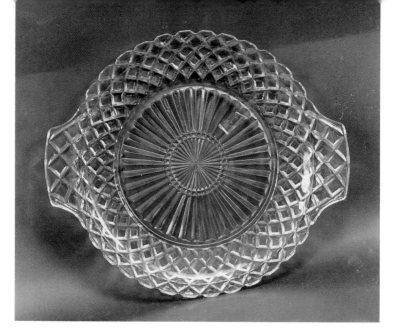

This handled cake plate in pink is not as plentiful as the crystal version. It is very appealing to collectors with the distinctive rim featuring the lattice or waffle design. This has radial sunburst lines and triple concentric circles of small blocks. Waterford, "Waffle," cake plate, handled, pink, 10-1/4", $16.

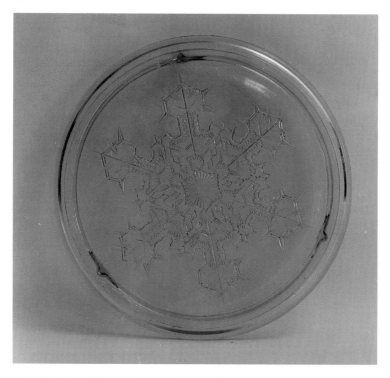

This type of cake plate with the large snowflake design and the groove around the rim for insertion of the lid is not too often seen. Snowflake cake plate, pink, 12-3/4", $30.

The Harp, a pedestal-type cake plate is the most unique of all the cake plates. There is a variety of them to collect and the search for them is challenging. Jeannette Glass Co. 1954-1957. **Left to right:** ice blue, beaded rim, 9", $34; crystal, flat rim with the harp design, 9", $22; crystal, with gold trim and harp design, 9", $22.

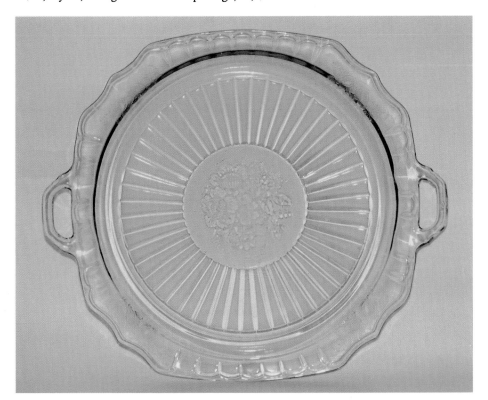

With its open loop handles this plate is unusual, but ideal for serving purposes. The center circle of roses, widely spaced radial lines, and the border of roses make a very attractive pattern. It is highly collectible. Mayfair, "Open Rose," cake plate with handles, 12", $33.

DEPRESSION GLASS IS NO. 1

After writing several articles on my favorites of Depression Glass, I thought I would briefly sum up the reasons I love this glass and why collecting it has become such an addictive and popular hobby.

First, I love the array of bright and bold colors. There are the different hues of pink (my favorite), the deep amethyst, bright ruby, spring green, and white opalescent. Then there is the cobalt blue with a mystique all of its own, lovely soft topaz, striking black, iridescent, royal blue, primrose yellow, amber lustre and the ever shining crystal. All of these colors truly represented the 1920s and 1930s.

Second, I love the variety of design. There are bubbles, ripples, radial sunbursts, scrollings, scallops and concentric circles. There are floral arrangements, cut and indented blocks, fruit motifs, spirals, swirled lines, spokes, and even a human figure? All of these characteristics truly give the glass a special charm.

Third, I love the shear numbers of patterns, from "Adam" to "Windsor Diamond." Each pattern has a unique design and a distinct name. The names are extremely interesting and fascinating because they are geographical like "Columbia," historical like "Windsor Castle", biblical like "Adam," and nature related like "Iris," "Orchid," "Lake Como," "Round Robin," and "Raindrops." The pattern "Miss America," one of my favorites and extremely popular with so many collectors, was named to capture the essence of American patriotism. I like the patriotic names like "Queen Mary" (sounds so British), and Coronation "Banded Fine Rib" Saxon (so royal and aristocratic).

Fourth, I love the functionality of Depression Glass, a piece produced specifically for the needs and eating habits of a particular time. Take for example the very popular grill plate, usually tri-sectioned and used in restaurants to keep the meat and vegetables divided from each other, while making small servings look more ample. "Tea Room," an early pattern made for restaurants and soda fountains, has the footed and ruffled sundae, that was so popular in the ice cream parlors. These tall tumblers I adore, as I do the banana-split boat.

One cannot forget the ever popular cookie jars, the beautifully shaped candy jars and covers, and butter dishes and covers. They have become such rarities today. Round bowls, called "nappies," in convenient sizes, were so popular for serving soups and sauces. Large pitchers for serving milk, water and other drinks, graced the center of the table. For the refrigerator there were popular stacking sets with one jar acting as a cover for the one below, and a handled cover on the top. There were the popular stemmed dessert dishes called sherbets and berry bowls, each used for serving a variety of foods. All of these had a specific purpose of the time.

Fifth, I love the nostalgic charm of Depression Glass. I grew up in the Depression Era and can vividly recall the sets of the colorful luncheon and dinnerware. And I remember how we got them. Attending a movie on a weeknight called the "dish night" and receiving a green dish. My parents purchased a bedroom and a living room "suite" at the local furniture store and received a free set of glasses or a set of dishes. Seed companies gave glassware away with the purchase of their seeds. Cereal bowls were found in cereal boxes and cake plates in bags of flour.

I love and collect Depression Glass because it sparkled in the homes of the Depression Era then and it sparkles anew in my home and other homes with intensifying popularity.

Spring green and pink cake plates. "Sunflower" pattern.

KNOW YOUR GLASSWARE

Is this piece an original, or a reproduction? This is the common and pertinent question being asked today among all collectors. Reproductions and reissues are becoming the main pitfalls of collecting Depression Glass. Believe me, I have found this to be true in my years of collecting.

Interest in Depression Glass is so lively that some contemporary glass companies have brought out new pressings from the old molds, or imitations of old patterns. There will always be some attempts by companies to reproduce this glass and thus take advantage of the collector. The fact that glass is very fragile creates a demand that is greater than the supply. With the number of collectors of Depression Glass unequalled in history, is it any wonder that reproductions will continue to plague collectors and saturate the field of collecting? Some of the most popular patterns like "Miss America", "Cherry Blossom", "Mayfair", "Sharon", "Cabbage Rose", "Cameo", and a few others are being reproduced, though only specific pieces are reproduced in some. There will always be unscrupulous individuals doing this, so watch out for them.

Glassware is easily reproduced and many copies have been proven to be misleading to the novice and the experienced collector alike. Reproductions often reach the dealers in some round about route and will be accepted and passed on as authentic because they were not aware of their existence. These pieces cause many problems in the collecting field, and especially if priced comparably with original pieces. Not only is it irritating to be duped, it can also be extremely expensive.

To prevent being victimized, become very knowledgeable of genuine Depression Glass. The library has a number of books on this subject, and the current information they offer on what is being reproduced is invaluable to collectors trying to accumulate meaningful collections. There is a great need for this information today.

Only a firm knowledge of true Depression Glass can help you avoid mistakes. You must have a certain instinct for Depression Glass and to acquire this you must study the glass first hand. There is considerable difficulty in determining the authenticity of glass, but through observation, thorough inspection, and close scrutiny the serious collector can distinguish a spurious piece from an authentic piece.

Haunting antique shops and attending shows where the glassware can be viewed, is an excellent way to become familiar with the special characteristics of the original pieces.

This newer jar is definitely larger than the older one of the same style, though, at first glance, one may think this jar is the original. The shape and design have similarities. I am very disappointed that there are re-issues of this beautiful glassware. In this case, I paid so little for this jar, that I do not feel cheated. I put it to good use every day. Now, I have acquired a firmer knowledge of the reproduction perils. "Sandwich," Anchor Hocking Glass Company 1939-1964. A reproduction cookie jar and cover, $10. New: 10-1/4" high, 5-1/2" opening width, 12" diameter (largest part). Old: 9-1/4" high, 4" opening width, 9" diameter, $35

Beginning collectors must depend on their research and, to a large extent, the integrity of the dealers when making their acquisitions.

After deciding what kind of Depression Glass pattern to collect or buy, familiarize yourself with your choice by reading specialized books and talk to well-informed dealers who are so willing to share their knowledge. Always try to deal with recognized dealers with reputations for honesty and reliability. View other collections whenever you can. Almost anyone is delighted to show their treasures. This not only gives you some important knowledge, it helps to establish a purpose and the contacts you need for building your collection.

Try to seek out the history of the pieces you collect. Talk to your grandparents and parents about Depression Glass. They love to reminisce about this and will know about the authenticity of the glassware.

The exchange of conversation and information can be extremely valuable in building a truly great collection.

TIPS FOR COLLECTORS

Have you been getting real bargains lately? Be careful in your answer; bargains can be expensive when they concern Depression Glass. A reproduction is usually less costly than an original. Be very cautious about the prices you pay. To all collectors of glass this is the first and sometimes the costliest lesson you will learn. To guard against the expensive bargain I offer the following suggestions.

Buying a piece of glass under poorly lighted conditions is unwise, unless you are prepared to be deceived. The true color of the glass and most defects are visible only under ideal lighting conditions. Examining glass in strong daylight rather than artificial light is very helpful to the collector.

Be extremely cautious about buying a dirty piece of glass; grime is an ideal camouflage for problems in the glass. I once bought a piece like this, against my better judgment. Fortunately, after a thorough cleaning, it turned out to be perfect. This is seldom the case. Clean the glass before you buy it.

Carefully examine pitcher handles, lips, rims and bases on the items. These areas will acquire a soft, warm appearance from use, and practically every piece of this glass will show some tell-tale maze of wear scratches. The surface of old glass possesses a soft dullness in comparison to the brilliant look of the newer glass. While wear is natural, beware of nicks and chips, which lower the value of a piece. Check the lips and handles of pitchers for nicks as these surfaces are extremely vulnerable.

Many pieces of glass, if tapped with a finger or an object like a pen, will ring and have an excellent tone due to the shape, thickness, and base. A bell-like ring often emanates from older glass. The lack of a ring may indicate a crack in the piece, and calls for a closer examination. Many pieces do not ring, so this doesn't always mean that a piece is bad.

The sense of touch can be very reliable in identifying original Depression Glass. With the daily usage of this glassware, the edges of the pieces will not be as crisp as new glass, being more rounded. Signs of scratching indicate normal use. A magnifying glass is imperative for scrutinizing glassware, and is an invaluable tool for any collector. Study marks which will help identify the outstanding characteristics. Learn the difference between traces of wear and the marks applied artificially to simulate wear.

The shapes of Depression Glass pieces can be confusing. In some patterns the sugar bowls do not have handles and thus resembles a footed tumbler or a sherbet. There is even a one-handled sugar bowl. It is wise to become very familiar with the typical look of the Depression Era look and style.

Colors play an important role in telling reproductions from the originals. Are the colors true to the patterns? Many pieces have come out in colors that were never made originally. The colors of reproductions are not as strong as the original glass, being much lighter and paler than the vivid original colors. Compare the colors and you will discern the difference. In the pink colors the original is a dainty, but intense pink. The reproduced color is more orange and generally much lighter. In the green color, the original is like a bright, fresh-looking green and in the reproduced color it is dull and paler.

Look for the impurities like bubbles, ripples, dents, small and large. These imperfections are characteristics of the original Depression Glass, and give it its special beauty.

Patterns play a significant part in distinguishing reproductions from the originals. The patterns in the various pieces reproduced are definitely weaker. In the reproduced cookie jars the design is very indistinct. On the bases of the items designs are less distinct with the original being more embossed. The molding marks are more distinct on old pieces than on the new. Some of the knobs on reproduced sugar lids, candy dishes and butter dishes are smooth whereas the old has a molded seam. There are often discrepancies in the shapes as well as in design. The moldings with roughness can greatly assist the collector in distinguishing the reproductions from the original. In reproductions there's variation in the sizes, and more crudeness in the shapes.

Look for a pontil, or mold mark. This can offer a clue to the pieces age and origin. The pontil mark, or scar, is a rough place on the bottom of the glassware where the pontil rod was attached. The pontil rod is a solid iron rod that supports the glass piece during the finishing process. After the piece is blown it is transferred from the blowpipe to the pontil rod for the final shaping and decorating. When completed, the pontil is broken away and the place where it attached is ground and reground and then polished to form a smooth circular depression. While the pontil mark can help identify an old piece, collectors must be wary. Sometimes the new mold for the reproduction has been made to look like an older mark. The pontil of the reproduction often is filled with bubbles and over all has a crude appearance, and is heavier than the old pontil mark.

Most of the reproductions are recognizable and can be easily detected by the person with a perceptive eye who knows what to look for. Remember the features: price far below the market, slight variations in size and patterns, weight comparison, the use of decoration and colors never used for the originals, lighter colors, weak designs in the pattern, and the absence of natural wear.

Again, to all collectors only a firm knowledge of true Depression Glass can help you in successful collecting and to avoid mistakes.

BE YOUR OWN GLASS DETECTIVE

A great glass collector must be a good detective. No piece of glass will be accepted at face value by a good detective. The wise collector looks for clues or characteristics that will prove the authenticity of a piece. Knowing what to look for can "make" or "break" a detective as well as a collection.

What are some of the traits of a good glass detective?

Patience is a most necessary trait for the glass detective. Rushing in wildly to buy is very unwise as this allows no time for identifying marks. Grabbing without keen observation is never a wise thing to do. One must always resist the sudden impulse that can lead to reckless buying of Depression Glass.

Courage, another good trait, can help the collector immensely to overcome the dealer's intimidations and become more confident in seeking out bargains.

Curiosity, a very important qualification, can spark the interest of the collector, raising questions of the origin and all of the characteristics of Depression Glass. Try to seek out the history as you collect. Talk to your grandparents and parents about your treasures. Seek out information from dealers especially at shows, flea markets, antique shops and at auctions.

Intuition, another important trait, can determine whether you will find an authentic piece of glassware when a quick decision has to be made. Always listen to your intuition, as this can be most helpful if you feel you don't have the adequate knowledge at the time. It may help you in finding a glorious "find."

Concentration is another valuable trait for the glass collector. Sometimes it is wiser to concentrate on one specialized field and do extensive research on your chosen subject. Concentrate on identification marks and study photographs of the glassware you want to collect. Buy several authentic pieces from reliable sources and use them for comparison.

Knowledge, this indispensable characteristic, is what determines a successful glass detective and collector. Become an expert by good reading. There are innumerable books and magazines available to collectors. Be sure to avail yourself of these.

With all of these traits and lots of experience, collectors develop a sixth sense in detecting authentic glassware. By developing them you will be able to collect more wisely, and will fully enjoy and appreciate the heirlooms you collect.

COMPANIES COLLECTORS SHOULD KNOW

Many companies produced Depression Glass. The most popular ones that collectors seek are Anchor Hocking of Lancaster, Ohio, Hazel Atlas of Clarksville, West Virginia, Federal of Columbus, Ohio, Indiana of Dunkirk, Indiana, Jeannette of Jeannette, Pennsylvania, and Macbeth Evans of Charlerol, Pennsylvania. These six companies produced most of the Depression Glass that is collected today. Setting up the plants for the production of tank glass was a very expensive financial venture. The smaller glass companies could not compete with the larger ones. This was very difficult for these firms especially during the Great Depression. However, at the start of the Depression, several glass firms were already in production with the tank glass items. Many of the patterns that are so popular today with collectors were produced for the first time in that fateful year, 1929.

Identifying Depression Glass by the manufacturer is another challenge facing collectors. Companies have their own trademark, which helps tremendously. The following is a brief history of the major Depression Glass manufacturers, followed by their trademarks.

Hocking Glass Company of Lancaster, Ohio, (early 1920s-1938), began making small wares. Anchor Hocking Glass Company was formed in 1937 in a merger. This company was the largest producer of Depression tableware. They supplied great catalog stores and large chain stores. Their designs ran the gamut from traditional Sandwich type to 1930s modern. The company is known for the great variety of pieces like ice tubs, reamers, steak plates and many more.

Hazel Atlas Company of Clarksville, West Virginia, (early 1930s), produced many of glass tableware services and much of the glass kitchenware that is now collected from the era of the 1920s and 1930s. Tumblers were produced in such abundance that the Clarksburg, West Virginia plant became known as the "World's Famous and Biggest Tumbler Factory". The green mixing bowl sets and the dinnerware in opaque white glass are highly collectible.

Federal Glass Company of Columbus, Ohio (1933-1937), produced a tremendous amount of Depression Glass. The major patterns collected today can be attributed to Federal. This company was outstanding in producing the machine pressed and mold-etched dinnerware in the popular array of colors. Some of the most popular patterns, like "Thumbprint," "Sharon," "Cabbage Rose," "Dutch Rose," "Raindrops," "Patrician," "Parrot," "Normandie," and "Mayfair," were produced by this company.

Indiana Glass Company of Dunkirk, Indiana (1926-1931), produced a limited number of mold-etched glass patterns in tableware in the early period of the Depression. Before this, Indiana produced pressed-glass tableware that they continued to make into the 1930s. Indiana identified their pattern with catalog numbers rather than names. This company is favored very highly among collectors for their serviceable crystal-ware produced for the soda fountains and tea rooms used extensively in the 1920s and then in color in the 1930s. "Tea Room," a early pattern made for restaurants and soda fountains, had thirty different shapes. This pattern represented the decorative art style, heavy pressed, geometric and flashy. "Pyramid," another heavy extreme art deco style, is another favorite of Indiana.

Jeannette Glass Company of Jeannette, Pennsylvania, (1935-1938), produced numerous patterns that are currently being collected. This company focused on traditional shapes and patterns in dinnerware. Its modern designs were typical of the artistic and decorative style of the era. It produced many beautiful colors and it will be remembered by all collectors for the exquisite mold-etched patterns and the typical Depression colors.

Fenton of Williamstown, West Virginia (1920s to the present), was instrumental in developing the iridescent colored ware. This is the Carnival glass collected today. Fenton has a beautiful line of vases, candlesticks, baskets, console sets, tableware, flower bowls and novelties in its exclusive colors.

L.E. Smith of Mt. Pleasant, Pennsylvania (1920s-1934), made numerous items in black glass during the Depression Era, as well as pink, green, amber, canary, amethyst and blue. This company is remembered mainly for the black glass, which is a collector's dream.

Cambridge, of Cambridge, Ohio (in the 1920s and 1930s), became known as the largest producer of American glass. The quality of glassware was superb and so was the color. Cambridge was the champion of color. After the company closed, the molds went to the Imperial Glass Company. This company introduced new shades, opaque color, swans and the very distinctive and famous table accessories.

The Westmoreland Company started to produce glass at Grapeville, Pennsylvania 1890. It produced specialties at first, but in the 1920s glassware of high quality was produced. The Early American patterns, were recreated and the production of milk glass began. This is still very popular today.

The Fostoria Glass Company (1928-1944), became the largest producer of quality glassware. Fostoria crystal was very distinctive and brilliant. All of the Fostoria patterns are very collectible today, but the colorful patterns from the Depression Era are highly treasured.

The McKee Glass Company of Jeannette, Pennsylvania produced much of the kitchenware items of the Depression Era. Color was strongly emphasized in the 1930s. This company was famous for the many opaque wares and crystal pressed patterns. The Prescut mark was first used around 1904. It is found with or without the circle and with slight variations. The mark without the circle is the oldest. These marks were in general use by McKee until the early thirties.

The United States Glass Company of Pittsburgh, Pennsylvania late 1920s, made a considerable amount of pink and green glass. This company produced the famous Shirley Temple pieces. The company was formed by the merging of 18 different glass factories in 1891. All of these various factories produced stemware and delicately pressed dinnerware.

Bartlett-Collins, (1931), began as a hand house, making utilitarian-pressed table items and lamp shades in crystal and open glass. Its lines of tableware from the 1930s are very collectible today. This company is best known for its production of kitchen lamps. All of these lamps were unique.

Heisey Company was established in Newark, Ohio and produced an abundant supply of handmade glass, the most popular ever seen or known in this country. The quality, workmanship and the vivid colors of this glassware has collectors searching widely for it. This company was widely advertised. The Heisy doors closed in 1956 and the molds went to the Imperial Glass Corporation.

The Diamond Glassware Company was short lived. In its brief operation, a high grade of handmade glass was manufactured in light cut and decorated tableware, and numerous novelties. Black appeared to be the popular color with gold and silver trims. Console sets and epergnes were a specialty of this company.

Imperial Company, (1920-1928), of Bellaire, Ohio, brought out the color with all its brilliance. The popular luncheon sets were produced by the thousands. Imitation cut glass (called Nu-Cut) in crystal and transparent colors was produced in the 1920s.

The Libbey Glass Manufacturing Company has a long history, but in the 1920s and 1930s, it produced a variety of tumblers and became famous for this. Libbey created the fine cuttings and artistic quality in glassware. Libbey produced all of the typical Depression Era colors. It is best known for its tumblers and the exquisite variety of glassware.

New Martinsville, too, has a long history, but in the 1920s and 1930s it brought out color and novel designs. Almost any item was produced in any color. Along with new colors came new lines of tableware designs. In 1944 the company was bought out and renamed the **Viking Glass Company** and is still producing glassware today.

Macbeth Glass Company of Charlerol, Pennsylvania, (1930-1932), was responsible for five of the major collectible Depression Glass tableware patterns that sold widely. It produced a lot of pink glassware and less of the other colors. "American Sweetheart" was the most popular pattern, along with the "S-Pattern," a very delicate and thin glass. Many of the patterns were daintier.

Duncan and Miller Glass Company of Washington, Pennsylvania (1936-1955), is known for its pattern glass and pressed wares. It will always be remembered for the crystal in the elegant line, and the famous swans produced in many sizes and colors after the war. In the 1950s, Duncan and Miller was sold to the United States Glass Company and the molds transferred to Tiffin, Ohio.

Much of the Depression Glass collected now was made in midwestern factories.

The companies would stress to customers that glassware is right, beautiful, useful, cheap and plentiful.

Wouldn't we collectors wish this were true today?

Company Trademarks

Anchor Hocking
Hazel Atlas
Federal
Indiana
Jeannette
Fenton
L.E. Smith
Cambridge
Westmoreland
Fostoria
McKee
US Glass
Bartlett-Collins
Heisey
Prescut by McKee
Diamond Glassware Co.
Imperial
Libbey
New Martinsville

COLLECTOR'S VOCABULARY LIST

Every collector of Depression Glass must have a thorough understanding of the terminology of this glass. You need to know more than the prices. A good understanding of the table settings of the past is a must. The words, "nappy", "salver", and "bon-bon" are totally unfamiliar to the novice collector.

Listed below are some of the common and significant Depression Glass terms.

Amethyst: a light pastel purple.

Amber: a brownish-yellow color.

AOP: an abbreviation for an "all over pattern".

Berry bowl: a small bowl usually 3 to 4 inches used for serving fruits, sauces and desserts. The large bowl is called the master bowl.

Bon-bon: a small, uncovered candy dish.

Bread and butter plate: a 6 inch plate for the bread and butter.

Bride's basket: an art-glass bowl in a silver-plated stand or frame used for display around 1900.

Butter ball or confectioner's dish: a tiny glass plate used for serving or a shallow glass which has a long center pole with closed handles at the top.

Butter dish: a covered dish, round or rectangular that held butter on the table.

Cake plate: a large flat plate with three short legs.

Camphor glass: frosted glass.

Candelabrum: a candlestick lamp stand, or chandelier with two or more branches.

Carafe: a bottle used for serving wine or water.

Cheese dish: similar to a covered butter dish with the bottom usually flatter.

Chop plate: a large serving plate.

Claret: a stemmed glass for serving claret wine.

Closed handles: solid tab handles.

Coaster: a glass liner sometimes used as an ash tray.

Cobalt blue: a dark, deep blue color.

Comport: a long stemmed dish for candy, fruit, etc.

Concentric rings: circles within circles.

Console bowl: a low oval bowl about 12 inches long. This was produced with a matching pair of candlesticks so the set could be used in the center of a long table.

Crackle glass: glassware with a surface resembling cracked ice.

Cream soup: a two-handled soup dish.

Crimped: a pinching effect on the top of a bowl or other dish.

Demitasse: a smaller than a normal cup with saucer.

Domino tray: usually a square tray-like piece made to hold the cream pitcher within the center ring surrounded by domino sugar cubes.

Ebony: a black color.

Epergne: an elaborate, tiered center piece consisting of a metal frame with dishes, vases, or candleholders made of glass, silver or porcelain made to hold ivy or flowers.

Etched: a design cut into the glass with acid.

Fake: to impart a false likeness.

Fired-on: color applied and baked on the dish.

Fluted: a scalloped edge.

Frog: a heavy glass with holes for holding flowers.

Goblet: a drinking glass with a stem.

Gravy boat: an oval shaped bowl for serving gravy with a spout.

Grill plate: a divided plate, usually large, introduced during the 1930s.

Hot plate: a glass plate used for placing hot items on the table for protection.

Jadite: an opaque, light green color.

Luncheon plate: an 8" or 9" plate, smaller than a dinner plate.

Mayonnaise bowl: an open cone shaped comport.

Milk glass: white opaque glass, usually heavy.

Mint: This is a common word any Depression Glass collector will hear over and over again. It refers to perfect, undamaged items with no scratches that looks as if it just came from a store. If the item is in the original box that definitely adds to the value. This is known as "mint in the box" and is the best a collector can hope for.

Monax: a white color.

Motif: the design on the glass.

Nappy: a round or oval dish with a flat bottom and sloping sides about 6 inches in diameter. An all-purpose dish used for puddings, ice cream, peas, apple sauce, or other juicy foods.

Opalescent: showing a display of colors like that of opal.

Parfait: a tall ice cream dish used for sundaes in soda fountains.

Platter: an oval or oblong shaped meat dish.

Rayed: spoke-like design on glass bottoms.

Reissue: to issue again.

Relish dish: an oblong pickle dish.

Reproduction: a likeness.

Reproduce: cause to exist again.

Rose bowl: a small, curved-in edged bowl.

Salad plate: a 7" to 7-1/2" plate for serving salads.

Salver: a round tray or platter on a high stem used for serving desserts or tea sandwiches.

Sandwich server: a center handled serving plate, or a salver.

Sherbet: a small, usually footed dessert dish.

Spoon holder: a vase-like container used to hold spoons on the dining table.

Stemmed Glasses: There are special names for stemmed glasses of various sizes and shapes; cordial, wine, claret, champagne and water.

Table set: a matching sugar bowl, creamer, spoon holder and butter dish.

Tid bit: a two or three layer serving piece with a metal upright and handle. Also called an hors-d'oeuvres plate or a cookie plate.

Topaz: a bright yellow color.

Trivet: a three-footed hot plate.

Tumbler: a drinking glass with no stem.

Ultra-marine: a blue-green color.

Water set: a pitcher with matching tumblers and, sometimes, a matching tray in cut or pressed glass.

Wine set: a decanter with matching wine glasses.

REFLECTIONS

Reflecting back on the years of the late 1920s and 1930s with the good and bad times, I'm so glad I grew up in that era. Many of my friends are puzzled about my deep feelings for this depressing period. Yes, the times were difficult with many unpleasant experiences which I'm sure most Americans would prefer to forget. However, the stamina, valor, courage and sacrifice displayed by the people has become a symbol of human endurance, unequaled in American history. I know because I was there.

When I think back of the beautiful rainbow table settings in the homes of the American people, I remember the important role color played in that era. Color was powerful, hopeful, fashionable, glamorous. Color was bursting out all over in the Great Depression. It was loved and appreciated, playing a tremendous part in lifting the spirits of the people's lives.

Color is still important. Everything in our lives reflects its influence. The changing of the seasons reflect the significant colors of green, orange, brown, rust, gold and white. The holidays strongly reflect colors like red, green, pink, blue and white. Fashions rotate around colors, as does home decor. Colors still play an important role in our lives, as they did in the 1920s and 1930s.

The glassware produced in the Depression Era cannot be mistaken for glassware made at any other time in American history. Who can forget the nostalgic ice cream parlors, featuring the tall stemmed glasses for the sodas and the banana split bowls for sundaes? This was a favorite of mine. The grill plates so unique, keeping the foods separate, have been replaced by the disposable paper plates and aluminum TV dinner trays. The popular cookie jars still remain a beauty and a necessity adding warmth to the kitchen. Mine are put to good usage daily. The variety of brightly colored bowls produced were so convenient for versatile serving and each one served with a specific purpose. Very attractive and refreshing were the tall pitchers in the cone shape (my favorite), filled with milk or lemonade on the center of the table surrounded by glasses. These sets were beautiful and useful and still serving the purpose today. Finding the various sizes of the glasses to match the pitcher is my challenge. These sets I love to display and use and are just as appealing today as in the 1920s and 1930s. The console set (bowl with matching candlesticks), still retain their glamour in our homes.

Reflecting back, I often wonder what would happen if our nation would suddenly be hit with a Depression like the late 1920s and 1930s. How would society cope with the hardships the hardy people endured back then? What product would come out of this period like the memorable Depression Glass?

DEPRESSION GLASS IS FOREVER

With the supply of this brilliant popular glassware dwindling and prices escalating, we must try to collect all we can to preserve these precious artifacts. Once gone they will always be gone. These pieces should instead become heirlooms for generations to come.

Remember that Depression Glass was every day glass early on and a lot of it was broken or discarded. Some was just stuck in the back of the kitchen cupboard. When the economy improved, Depression Glass was somewhat forgotten in favor of higher quality glassware.

Depression Glass has become a symbol of a less complicated way of living. Paying so little for this glassware and getting so much in return is truly something to be memorable in this day and age.

This glassware of the 1920s and 1930s is still available because some of it was made in huge quantities. In general it is becoming more expensive and scarcer. Plates, bowls and tumblers costing pennies then, now cost many dollars, yet some pieces are quite affordable compared with the astronomical cost of other antiques. As the old saying goes, you can still buy this special glassware without hocking your family's jewels. However, this may not always be so, with prices soaring to the four-digit range. Many collectors are picking up all of the Depression Glass they can find because some of the patterns are reaching the endangered species level. The search is intensifying for all types of this glassware.

Depression Glass holds a very special place in my heart. Growing up in the Depression era is the reason for my intense love of this precious glassware. I was intrigued from the start due to its brightness of colors and shapes and I am still intrigued today.

My many years of collecting have been the most memorable period in my life. My only regret is that I didn't discover this world of searching, researching, endless hunting and great fun, earlier. It has taken me to places I never dreamed of. Perhaps the greatest reward is the wonderfully unforgettable friendships that have developed. As I have found out, Depression Glass people are very down-to-earth, congenial, and just good people. All have these things in common; their enthusiasm, willingness to share, and preservation-mindedness.

What better way to spend our retirement years than with a house filled with colorful, sparkling and diverse Depression Glass. Not a day goes by that we don't enjoy its beauty by viewing it, using it, decorating our house with it, or researching it. Our house is a "rainbow" with each room decorated around the display of the individual colors of this glassware. And the colors change with the seasons. In December, red and green make their annual appearance, with red and green vases adorning the window sills, and the Christmas table setting in green and red. It is very festive looking, and my family enjoys it, looking forward to it each year.

A piece of Depression Glass with its glittering color, unique shape, and striking ways in which it reflects light, is a joy forever. This glassware will never be forgotten; it will be admired and sought after for centuries.

As I tell my friends—there is nothing depressing about Depression Glass, it sparkles anew with increasing popularity.

The motto, "Eat it up, wear it out, make it do, or do without" would have a tremendous impact on the majority of the American people. In reality, would we as a nation be able to make the enormous sacrifice? In our affluent society, would we actually survive? Perhaps the word depression would take on a different meaning and the experience would be nothing but depressing.

In summarizing, the great virtues and heirlooms of the Depression Era, along with the values, are unforgettable.

These are some of the accessory pieces in Royal Ruby used during the Christmas holidays. Anchor Hocking produced the Royal Ruby in the 1940s. All of these add a festive touch. **Left to right:** vase, 6-3/8", $6; vase, 3-1/2", $4; bon-bon, footed, 6-3/4", $10; handled tray, 7", $10.

These Serva-snack sets in the crystal fan are very popular at Christmas with the red and green cups. Fan crystal, 10-1/4", width of indent, 7-3/4", $8. Cups, green and red, 5 oz., $3.

These are some of the accessory pieces in Forest Green used during the Christmas season. Anchor Hocking produced the Forest Green in the 1950s, and it, too, is very festive, blending well with the red. **Left to right:** bowl, 5-1/2", $6; vase, 3-1/2", $4; vase, 6-3/8", $6; flared bon-bon, square footed, 6-3/4", $6.

The Royal Ruby salad bowl and the salad plate is a very beautiful combination. This is one of the first pieces to make its annual appearance in December and makes an attractive centerpiece. Both are becoming difficult to find. Salad bowl, 11-1/2", $32. Salad plate, 13-3/4", $35. This plate is scarce.

The Royal Ruby punch bowl and the cups are a beauty to display and use. At Christmas this holds our traditional punch. I'm searching for the stand for the punch bowl, which is difficult to find. Punch bowl, without base, 9-3/4" to 10", $40. Cups, 5 oz., set of 10-12 cups, $3 each cup.

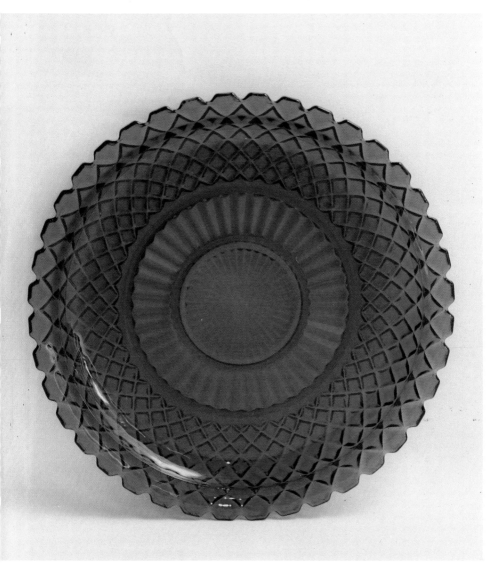

This is another attractive serving piece in green. I use this plate for Christmas cookies. It can also be used for serving snacks in the white or crystal inserts. Waterford "Waffle" sandwich plate, Forest Green, 13-3/4", $12.

BIBLIOGRAPHY

Florence, Gene. *The Collector's Encyclopedia of Depression Glass*. Paducah: Collector's Books, 1996.

Huxford, Sharon and Bob. *Schroeder's Antiques Price Guide*. Paducah: Collector's Books, 1996.

Kovel, Ralph and Terry. *Antiques and Collectibles Price List*. New York: Crown Publishers, Inc., 1996.

Rinker, Harry L. *Warman's Antiques and Their Prices*. Radnor, PA: Wallace-Homestead Book Co., 1995.

Steel, Teri, Editor. *The Daze,* monthly newspaper. Otisville, Michigan.

Weatherman, Hazel. *Colored Glassware of the Depression Era 1*. Ozark, Missouri: Weatherman Glassbooks, 1970.

_____. *Colored Glassware of the Depression, Era 2*. Ozark, Missouri: Weatherman Glassbooks, 1974.